IMAGES
of America

DUQUESNE

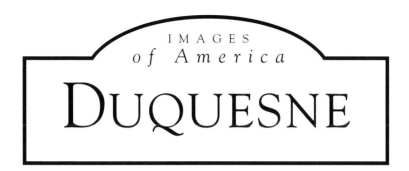

IMAGES
of America

DUQUESNE

Daniel J. Burns

ARCADIA

Copyright © 2005 by Daniel J. Burns
ISBN 0-7385-3772-1

First published 2005

Published by Arcadia Publishing,
Charleston SC, Chicago IL, Portsmouth NH, San Francisco CA

Printed in Great Britain

Library of Congress Catalog Card Number: 2004117629

For all general information, contact Arcadia Publishing:
Telephone 843-853-2070
Fax 843-853-0044
E-mail sales@arcadiapublishing.com
For customer service and orders:
Toll-free 1-888-313-2665

Visit us on the Internet at www.arcadiapublishing.com

CONTENTS

ACKNOWLEDGMENTS

I would like to thank all those who made this book possible through their donations of historic photographs to the Homestead Mifflin Township Historical Society. Special thanks go to the keepers of Duquesne history: William Gallagher, Bill Hensler, Dom Toretti, Jim Hartman, and the late Joe Walker. I would also like to thank John Armstrong from U.S. Steel for his support. Last but certainly not least, my most sincere gratitude goes to my dearest Sarah. Without her support and assistance, this project would have never been a reality.

INTRODUCTION

In 1891, just before the turn of the 20th century, a local newspaper described Duquesne as a town that had "dropped its swaddling clothes and entered a new age. . . . We have seen transformation from a village community to a prospective hustling and bustling borough." With its incorporation as a borough, Duquesne was well on its way to leaving a permanent mark on the map of American industrialization.

For the next eight decades, Duquesne gained a reputation in the manufacturing community as a steel-producing giant, contributing to both world wars and to the industrial expansion of the United States both at home and abroad. It was a town with a rough and gritty exterior, but it was a place that always put community and family above all else. It was a town where people worshiped and attended church faithfully, where neighbors took care of and watched out for one another.

Duquesne is a town that honors those who served, those who sacrificed themselves and their lives in service to their neighbors and their country. It values its history and marks its anniversaries with celebration and pride.

While compiling the images in this book, I found that there was no shortage of people eager to share a photograph or a story about what was, about where something once stood, or about who did what. Like most towns and communities, this town has seen its share of good times as well as bad. No matter what the topic of discussion is about the town, however, Duquesne is always spoken about with pride by the people who have lived, worked, and shopped within its borders.

One
PIONEERS AND SETTLERS

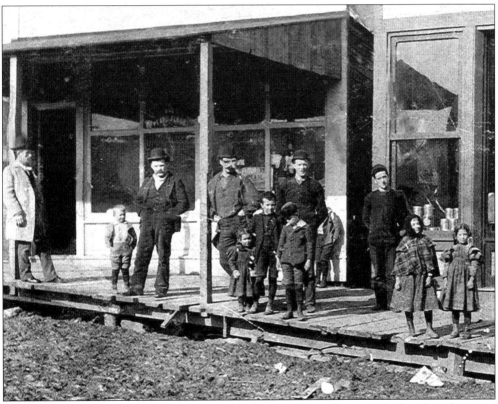

Located seven miles from Pittsburgh in Allegheny County, Duquesne's abundant farmland eventually became a yearly meeting place for Methodists from all over the eastern seaboard. An early settler was once quoted as describing the land in the area as "God's choice." In 1893, the business center of Duquesne, Grant Avenue (pictured above), was no more than a handful of shops, including a butcher, a dry goods store, and a barbershop.

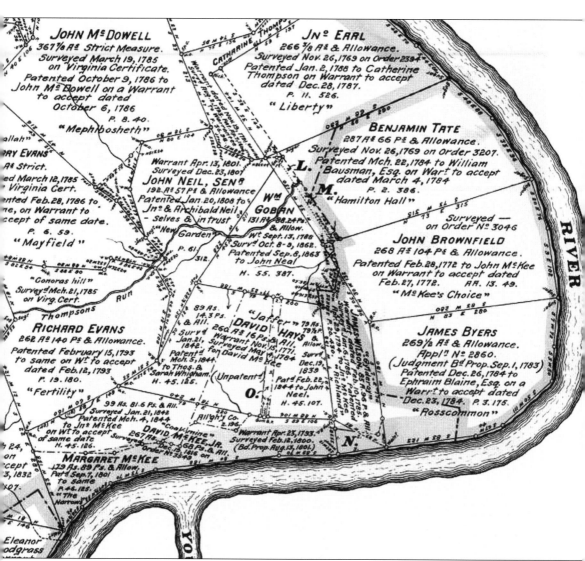

Benjamin Tate filed the first land patent for what is now Duquesne on April 3, 1769, at the newly opened land office in Pittsburgh. The tract was known as Hamilton Hall and spanned nearly 290 acres. A year later, Tate transferred the property to Gen. William Thompson. In April 1791, it was transferred to Peter Charles DeLuziere, a Frenchman.

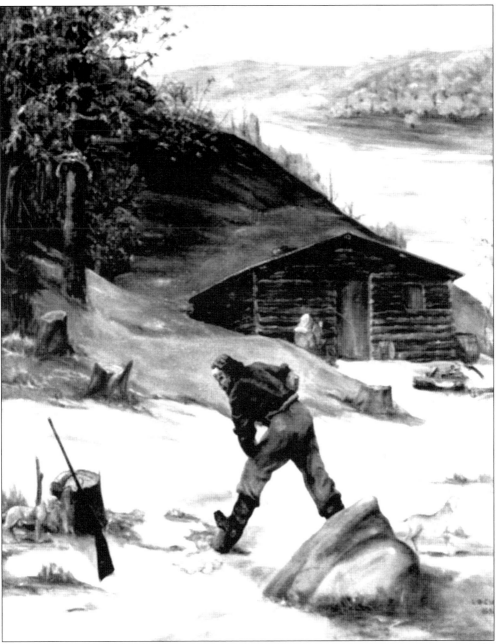

This portrait of Benjamin Tate depicts the pioneer as the first settler in the Duquesne area. The artist, Levi Claggett, was the first African American child born in Duquesne and the first to graduate from what is now Carnegie Mellon University. The original painting hangs in the council chambers of city hall.

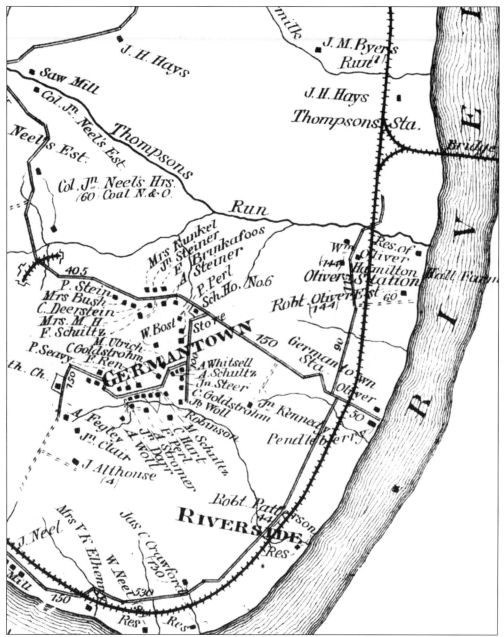

By the early 1800s, John Neel had opened the area's first gristmill, which ground the corn and rye grown by neighboring settlers. Within a few years, a dozen houses were built in the area. Made mostly of logs, these homes belonged to families whose names are known in the area to this day: Gallagher, Mehaffey, Oliver, Goldstrohm, Zewe, Wool, Cochran, and Crawford, among others.

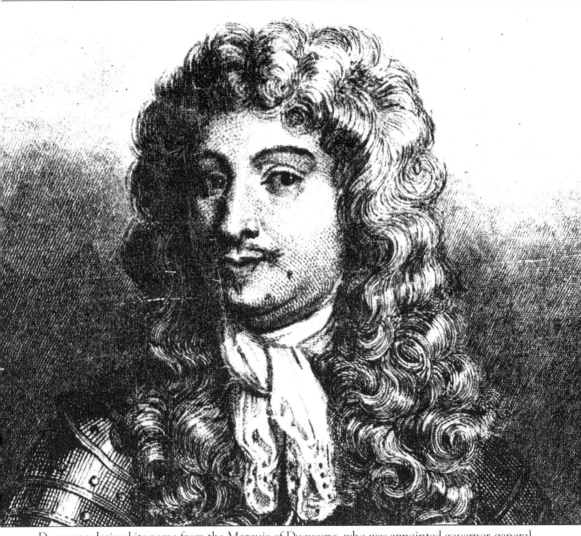

Duquesne derived its name from the Marquis of Duquesne, who was appointed governor-general of Canada by King Louis XV of France and served from 1752 to 1755.

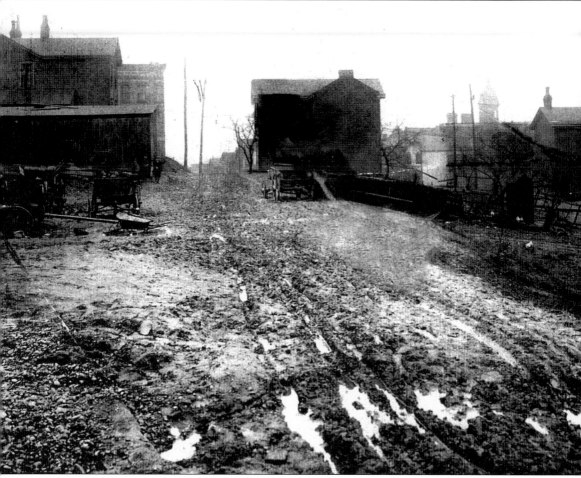

The unpaved streets were well traveled by horse and by cart, leaving a muddy soup after even a light rain. A colleague once asked W. J. Dorsey, a Duquesne attorney, "How do you people get around up there?" Dorsey replied, "We get around as best we can. Everybody wears gum boots. The men wear them, the women wear them and the children wear them. I can tell a Duquesne man, woman or child anywhere if I can get a look at their feet."

Two

A TOWN
FORGED IN STEEL

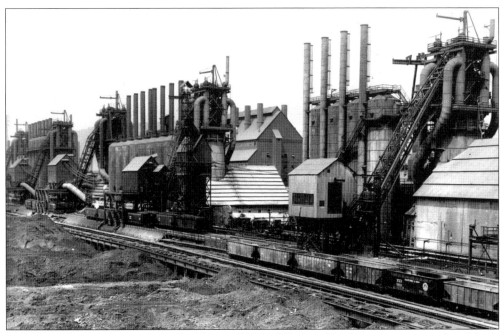

In 1886, a few employees from the National Tube Works of McKeesport organized and built another tube mill operation. The Duquesne Tube Works Company began production in 1887, boasting $100,000 in capital stock and employing approximately 100 men. Within three years, the employment roster grew to nearly 500, and the company was producing 150 tons of tubes and pipes per day. In 1896, the plant was forced to close due to financial problems. The Carnegie Steel Company built a new mill on the site of the old tube works in 1901.

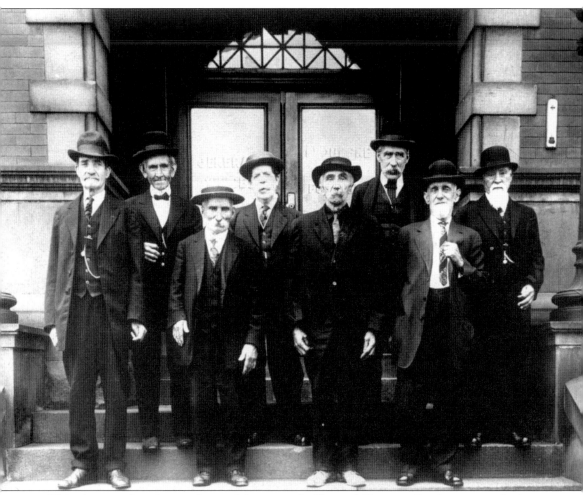

This photograph, taken in front of the general offices of Carnegie Steel, captures Andrew Carnegie (far right) during one of his many known visits to Duquesne. During his first visit, in November 1898, Carnegie toured the facility and inspected the new 16-inch continuous mill. Carnegie also took time to meet with the recently formed library committee, pledging that he would give the town a library as fine as the one he had built in Homestead. Unfortunately, there is no record of the date or reason for Carnegie's last visit to Duquesne before his death in August 1919.

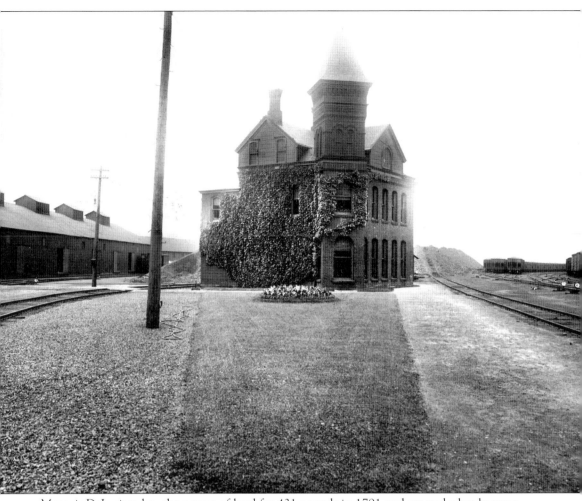

Marquis DeLuziere bought a tract of land for 431 pounds in 1791 and erected what became known as the Oliver Homestead. DeLuziere was a man of wealth who employed many local residents. His butler, Anthony Dravo, was the grandfather of John F. Dravo, who became known as a great riverman and who founded the town of Dravosburg.

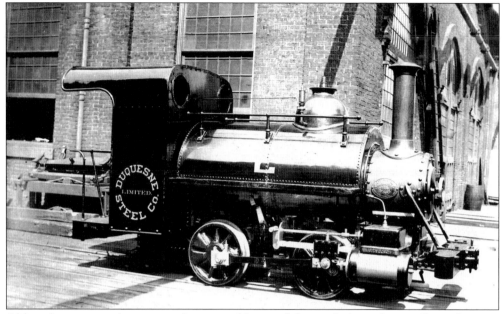

Although it was not known as a heavy workhorse of the steel plant, this small runabout, or dinkey engine, pulled more that its own weight, transporting men, materials, and small machinery from one side of the facility to the other. This engine was built locally at the Pittsburgh Locomotive Works in 1897.

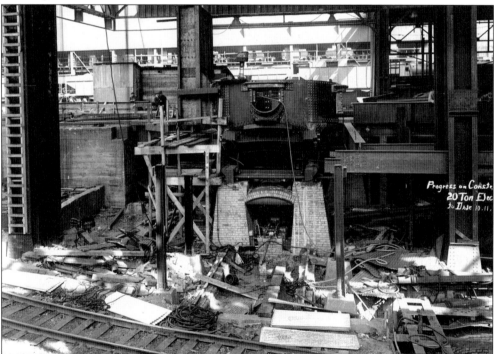

Depicted here is the construction of the 20-ton electric blast furnace. It was one of four units in the plant; each had the capacity to process 2,500 tons of material every 24 hours. The furnaces worked in groups of two, each having four stoves, a cast house, and a boiler plant.

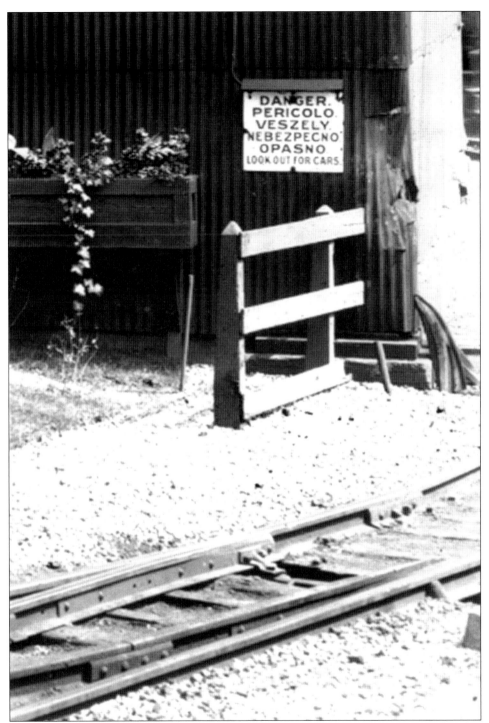

At the turn of the 20th century, the mill employed men from all over the world, including immigrants from nearly every country in Western Europe who had come to America to join the growing industrial labor force. A sign posted at an intersection with railroad tracks demonstrates this vast diversity as it warns of danger in five different languages.

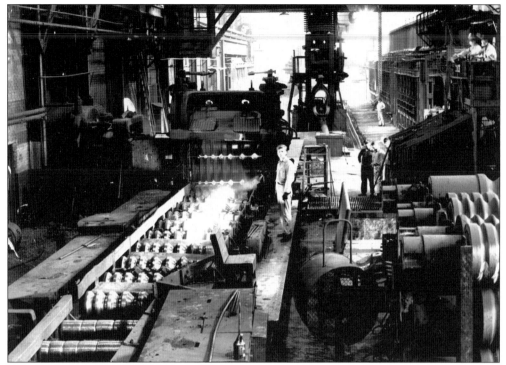

One of the plant's rolling mills was kept in motion by two 2,000-horsepower engines. Liquid steel was poured into ingots and rolled out to form billets, blooms, or sheet bars. The finished product was then removed to storage yards by one of three 10-ton cranes.

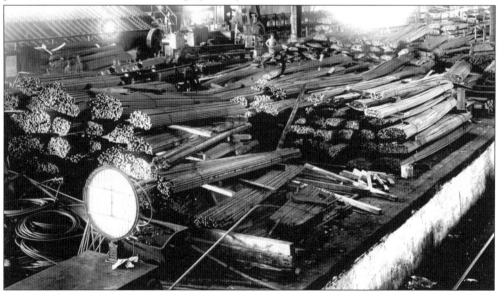

Carnegie Steel, one of two merchant mills on site, maintained a 10-inch mill and a 13-inch mill. Both mills produced round, flat, and angled steel that was used to make a variety of products, from farm implements to steel bridges, viaducts, and buildings. The 10-inch mill had an estimated annual production of about 45,000 tons, and the 13-inch mill produced about 110,000 tons annually.

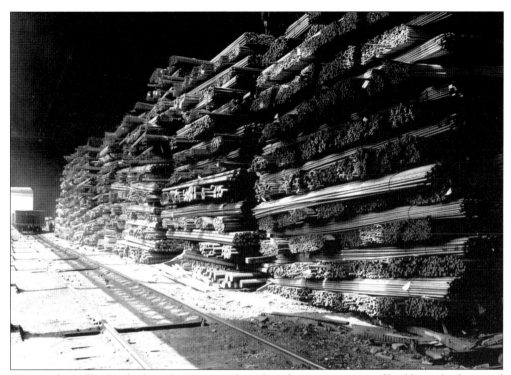

Among the mill's finished product was steel used in the construction of buildings, bridges, and railroads and in concrete reinforcement. It was also used to make products for military applications such as armor, tanks, artillery shells, and bullets.

Virtually a city within itself, the Carnegie Steel mill was a self-supported operation; all of the facilities it needed to function were located on site. These facilities included a water treatment plant, chemistry and metallurgy labs, a small hospital, and a carpentry shop (shown here).

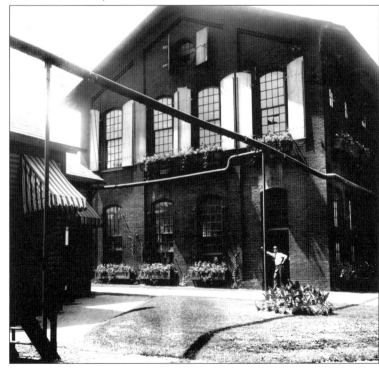

21

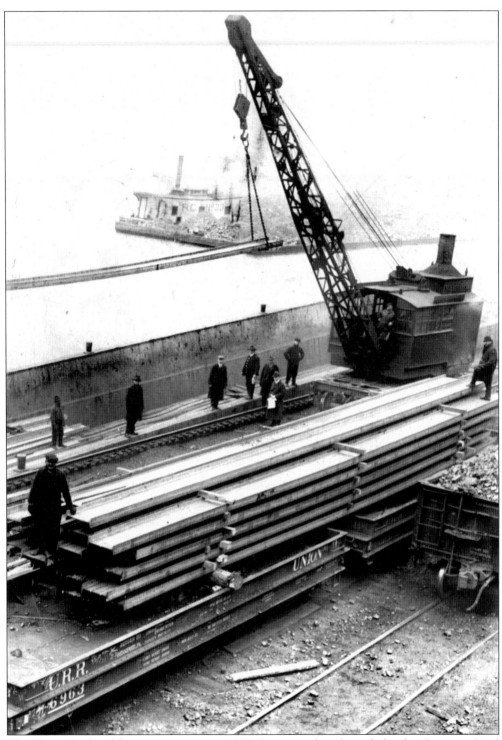

The Union Railroad began operations in 1898. It was used exclusively by the Carnegie Steel Company for the transportation of materials among the steel-making operations in Duquesne, Homestead, and Braddock.

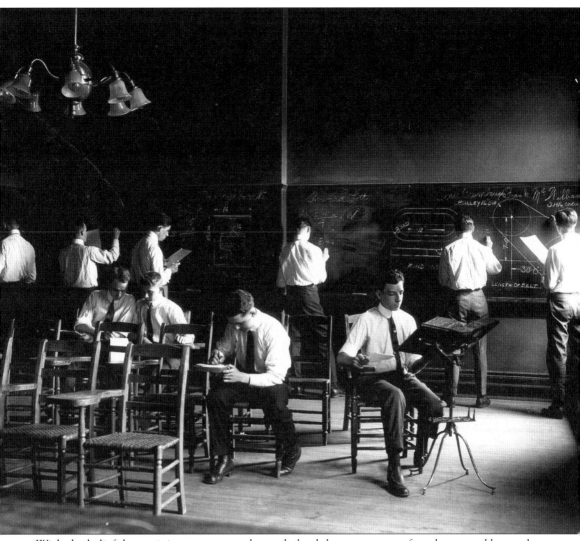

With the belief that training current employees helped the company perform better and boosted production, Carnegie Steel offered classes in English, drafting and drawing, and mathematics (shown here). Many of the students were immigrants with little or no prior education.

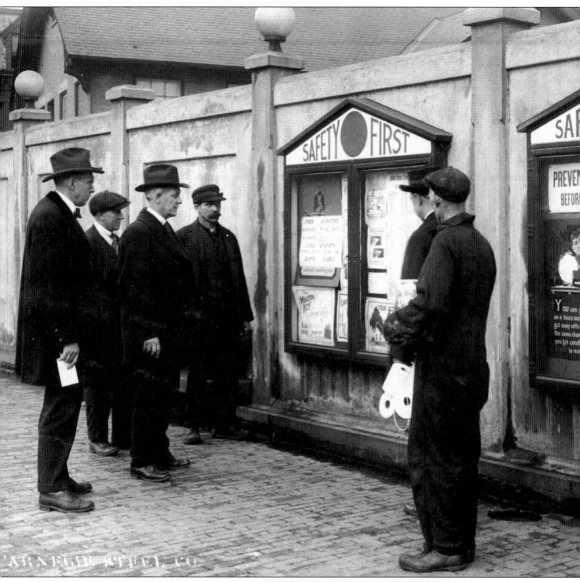

Plant executives and employees alike examine the the company's bulletin board promoting plant safety. It is easy to tell the difference between the executives and the labor force in this photograph; the decision makers rarely got their shoes dirty or scuffed. The man on the right appears to be the replenisher of the toilet paper.

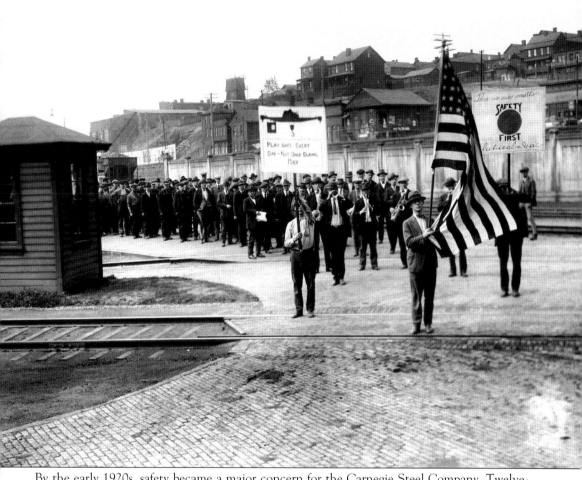

By the early 1920s, safety became a major concern for the Carnegie Steel Company. Twelve-hour days and six-day workweeks were taking their toll on the workers and the plant. Industrial accidents claimed the lives of workers at a rate of up to five per week. Accidents occurred not only within the plant but also in the rail yards. After Carnegie Steel initiated its Safety First accident-prevention program, fatalities and plant injuries were dramatically reduced. Employees participate in a spring safety parade with the theme "Play it safe everyday, not just in May."

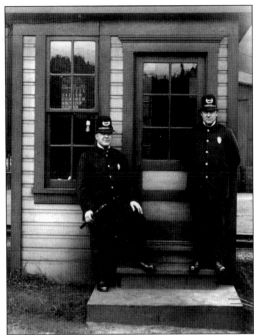

The Carnegie Steel Company, like many industrial organizations, employed its own security force. The responsibility of these internal police officers was to keep the peace, guard against trespassers, and prevent theft. These men were known to use a heavy hand and a large stick.

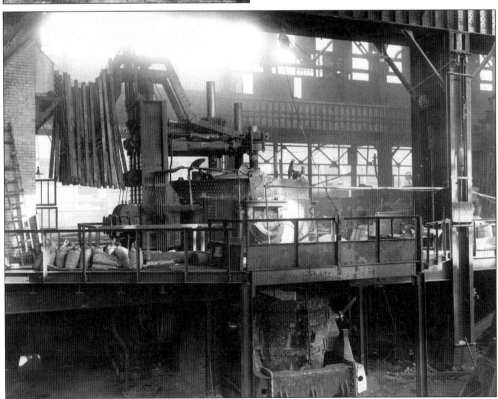

In 1901, Carnegie Steel became a subsidiary of U.S. Steel, erecting two additional bar mills and an open-hearth furnace. Within five years, an additional bar mill, the roll shop, and a car dumper were built to boost the already fast-paced production.

Shown here is one of three 75-ton traveling cranes that moved ladles of molten steel to the pouring building, where the giant buckets were overturned and the material was poured into ingots.

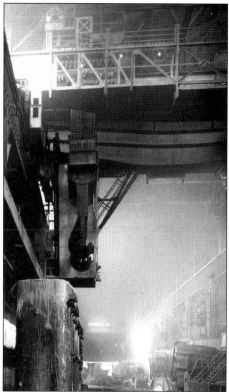

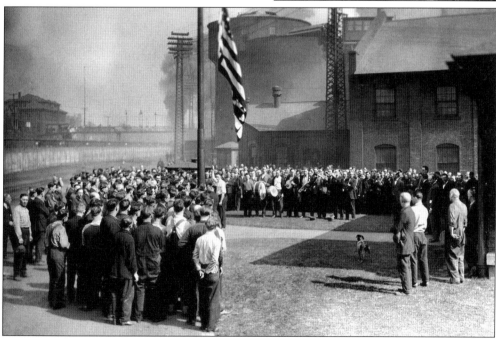

At an early morning flag raising, with the Carnegie Steel Company Band in attendance, company supervisors and employees show their patriotism. Such gatherings also provided an opportunity for mill managers to address employees on safety and production matters.

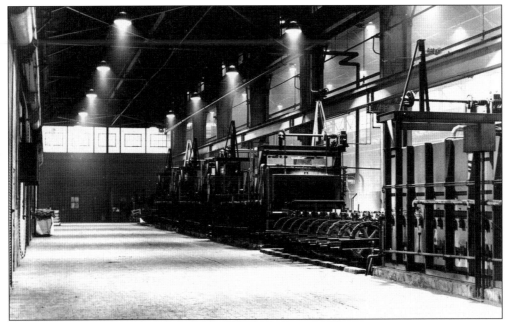

The plant's electrical department consisted of five 500-horsepower generators and housed its own 10-ton crane. The facility had an internal chemistry lab with a chief metallurgist who conducted industry-leading experiments on ore, iron, slag, and steel.

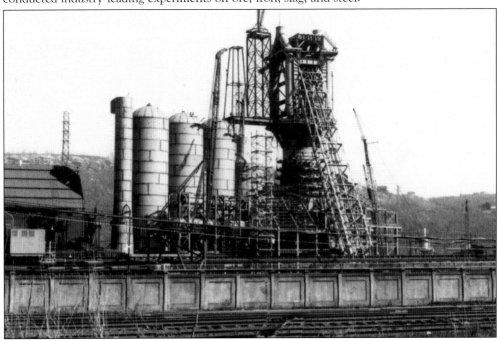

The continuous mill process is best defined as a series of mills and machinery placed in line to manufacture a more complete product. Because Carnegie Steel utilized this method, in one year the Duquesne Works reduced nearly 1.4 million tons of ore in the production of steel. This material was transported in 96,000 train cars; if these cars were coupled together, they would make up a train nearly 1,500 miles long.

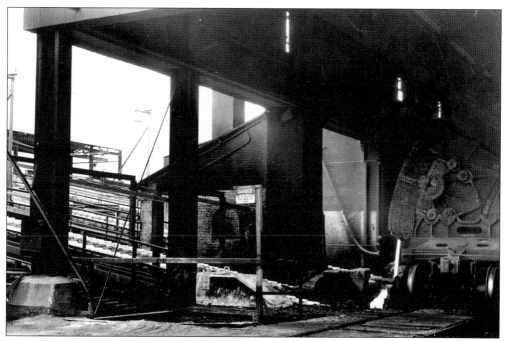

The railroad system of the steel plant was truly the lifeline of the production process. There were over 25 miles of railroad tracks within the complex. The constant movement of materials and finished products using 6 to 8 large locomotives and 20 dinkey engines was a logistical marvel and often a safety nightmare.

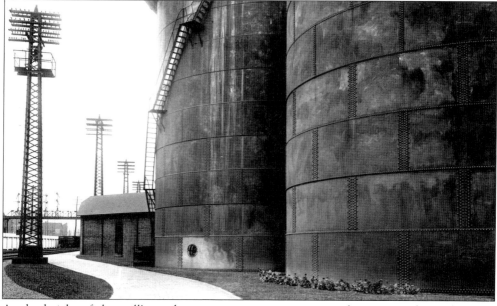

At the height of the mill's production, an enormous amount of water was drawn from the Monongahela River at a rate of nearly 31 million gallons a day. The water was utilized for hydraulic pressure, to keep the furnaces cool, and to maintain the plant's boilers. Before being used in many of these applications, the water had to be filtered, softened, and stored for use, as shown here.

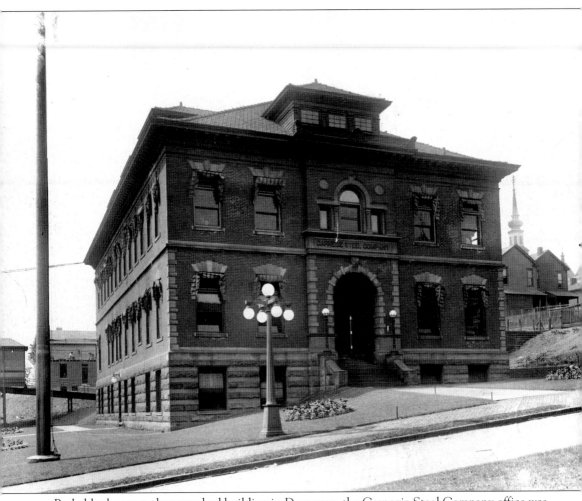

Probably the most photographed building in Duquesne, the Carnegie Steel Company office was constructed along Library Street and Duquesne Avenue. It housed the offices of the mill superintendent and the plant supervisors. The building served Carnegie Steel and U.S. Steel; it now stands as part of the Duquesne Innovation Center for technology and development.

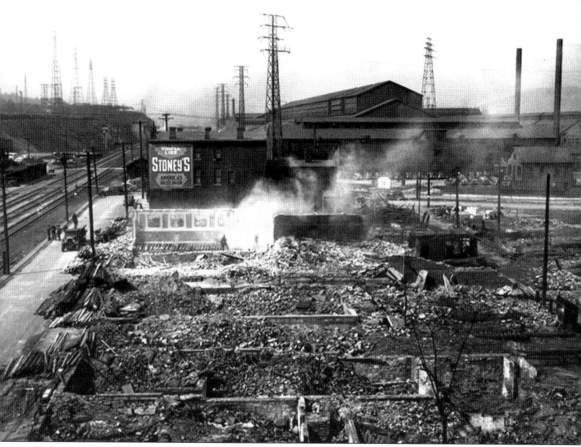

In June 1941, the Carnegie-Illinois Steel Corporation expanded the site by building a $10 million defense plant for the war effort. Thirty-eight acres of land were redeveloped for mill usage, eliminating over a dozen streets and alleys from the map and displacing nearly 200 families. The land was purchased from the Oliver family at a reported cost of $2 million.

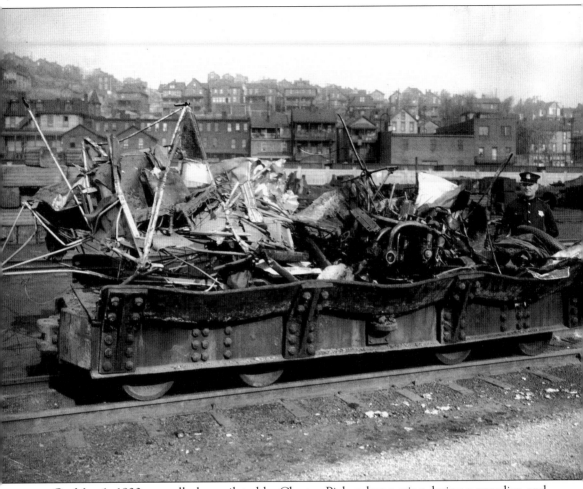

On May 1, 1930, a small plane piloted by Chester Pickup lost a wing during a nosedive and crashed. The aerial maneuver had been requested by the plane's passenger, who believed that a high nosedive would relieve his partial deafness. Both men parachuted to safety, but the plane crashed into the No. 1 open-hearth furnace building, damaging part of the roof. The aircraft was removed from the roof by a crane and placed in a railroad car.

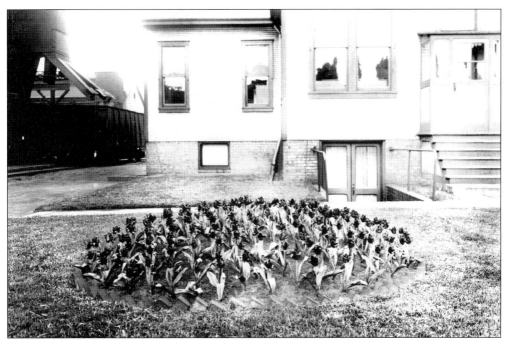

The year 1916 saw the erection of the physical testing laboratory, the No. 7 bar mill, the 20-ton electric furnace, and the electrode factory. In addition to producing steel for the expansion of America, the Carnegie Steel Company played no small role in World War I.

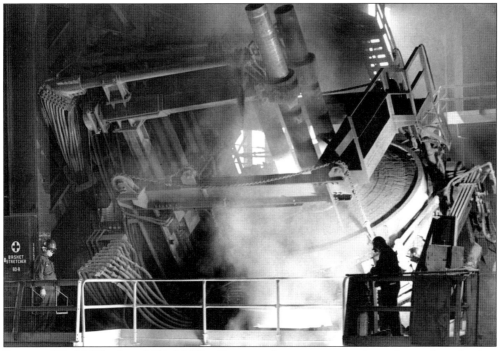

Between World War I and World War II, many changes were made to the steel production process. One of these changes was the introduction of a preheating process that produced a high-quality product that was very much in demand as America's need for steel products increased.

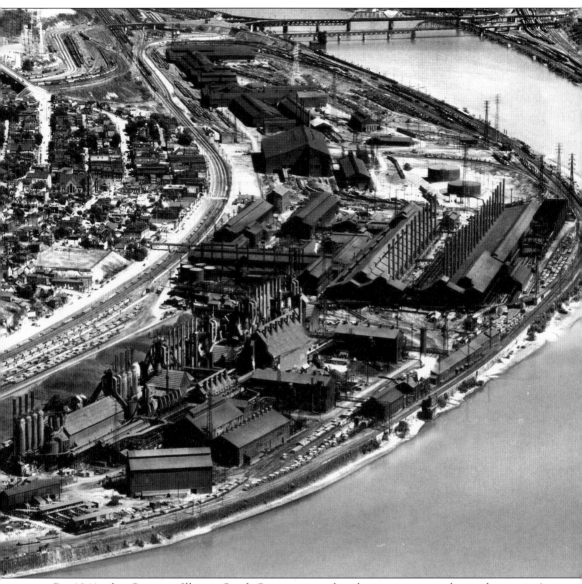

By 1941, the Carnegie-Illinois Steel Corporation played a prominent role in the nation's defense. Later under the control of U.S. Steel, the Duquesne Works was a city within a city. Covering no less than 250 acres, it maintained its own power plant, water treatment facility, and railroad transportation system. It also included a machine shop, a blacksmith and carpenter's shop, and four boiler houses.

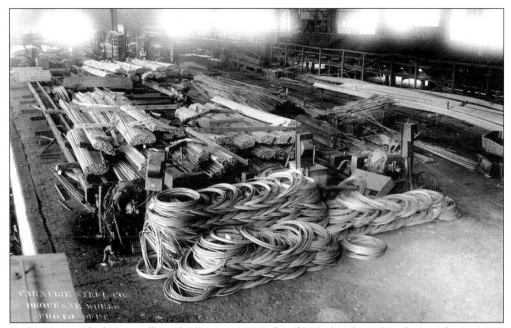

To keep up with the war effort, the Duquesne Works of U.S. Steel employed more than 10,000 men and women. The employees contributed to the production of steel used in the manufacture of bullets, artillery shells, and armor.

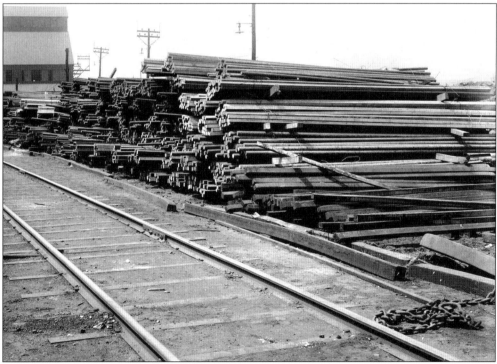

At the height of steel production in Duquesne, the merchant mills produced an annual total of nearly 155,000 tons of product, the 10-inch mill produced about 45,000 tons, and the 13-inch mill cranked out about 110,000 tons.

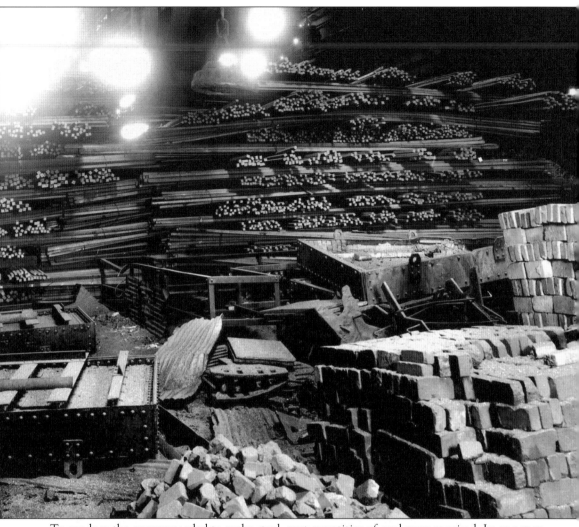

To produce the energy needed to make steel, vast quantities of coal were required. In one year alone, 542 barges were off-loaded at the plant's coal dock. This number represents 22.6 million bushels or 222 acres of product consumed by the mills on an annual basis.

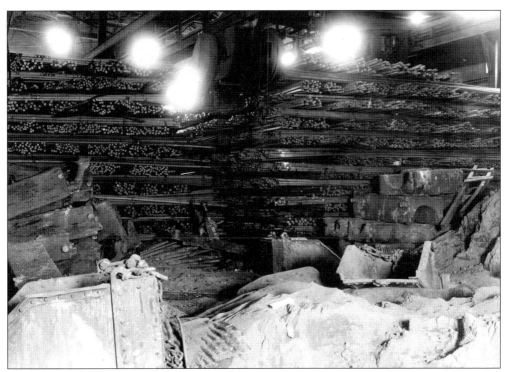

Before the 1920s, the average steelworker put in a 12-hour shift seven days a week. By 1930, U.S. Steel had reduced shift lengths to between 8.5 and 10.5 hours for most of its employees. The average worker also received an 80¢-a-day raise, increasing the pay from $4 to $4.80 a day.

In 1920, U.S. Steel offered health and accident insurance, pension plans, and housing assistance to its employees. The programs were a benefit not only to the Duquesne workers but also to employees at all of the company's production facilities.

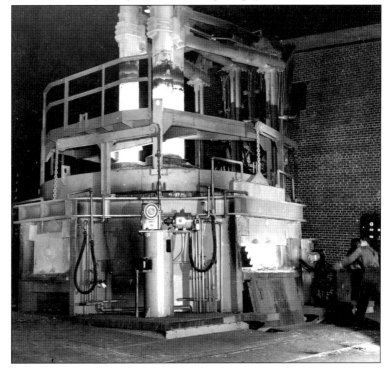

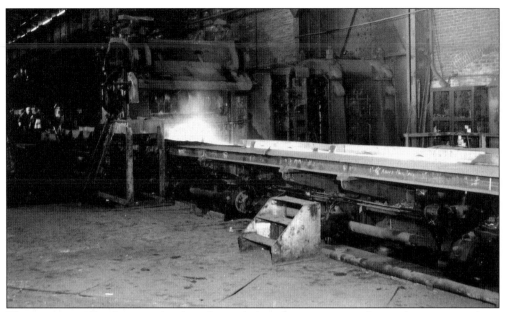

The company offered many other benefits including the opportunity for employees to purchase stock options. The purpose of this benefit was mainly to keep employees interested in their work and to encourage them to remain loyal to the company.

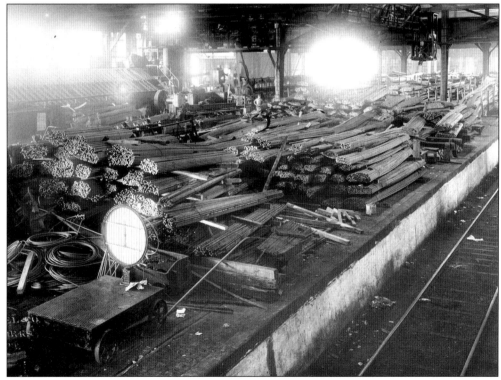

Even with the advent of safety policies and initiatives, injury and death continued to plague the facility, although not on the scale of years past. Employees were crushed by train cars on the railroad, burned and asphyxiated at the blast furnaces, and drowned in the river at the coal docks.

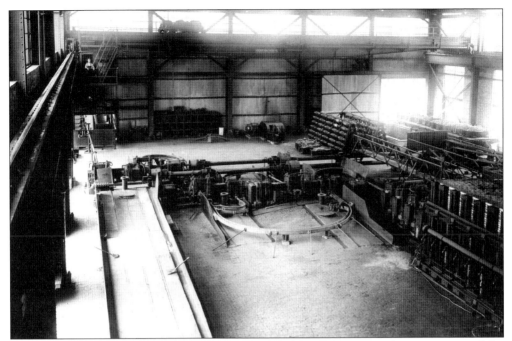

The machine shop contained all of the tools needed for the repair and maintenance of the mill's equipment, including drill presses, boring machines, and lathes. The shop also had a 20-ton overhead crane for moving equipment.

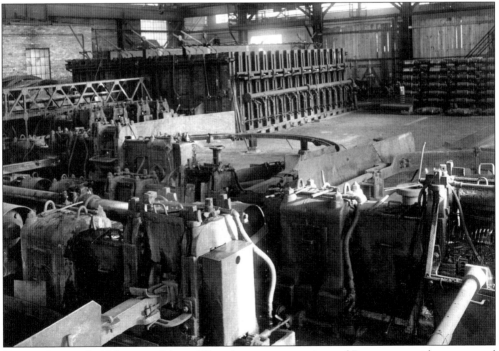

During the nearly 100 years of the mill's existence, generations of Duquesne residents sweated and worked to produce steel that was shipped and used the world over. Many times it was said that the quality of Duquesne's steel product was exceeded only by the pride of its workers.

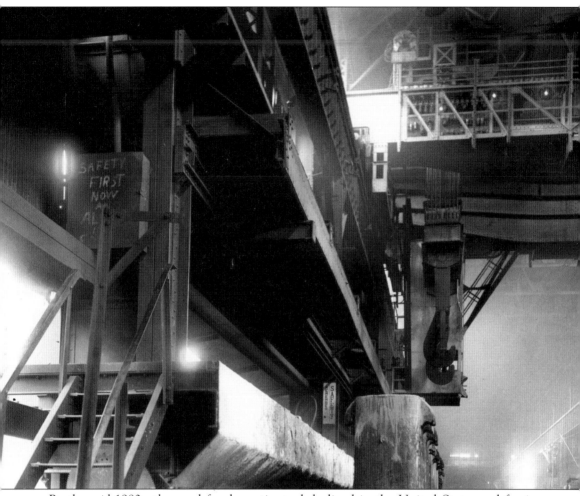

By the mid-1980s, the need for domestic steel declined in the United States and foreign countries could produce a cheaper product. These facts prompted the closing of the Duquesne Works and other steel plants in Pittsburgh and around the country. What was once a powerful machine that employed thousands and contributed to two world wars now lay dormant and quiet.

Three
A True Community

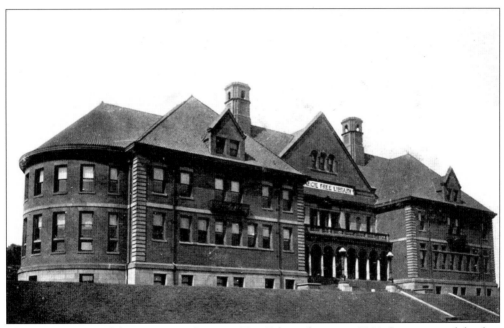

The construction of the Duquesne Carnegie Free Library began in 1901. It was one of the first of over 2,500 libraries built by Andrew Carnegie throughout the world. After being sold to the school district, the library was torn down in 1968 to make way for a school annex. It was determined, however, that the annex project would result in lost revenues for the district, and the plan was scrapped. Houses now occupy the site where the mammoth library once stood.

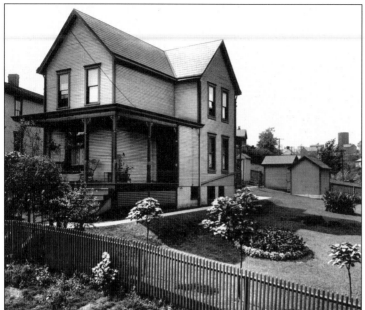

Among the many programs initiated by the Carnegie Steel Company was the annual City Beautiful Contest. Every spring, the mill photographers would go out into the community and photograph the houses, yards, and gardens of mill employees. The company awarded prizes in the categories of best-decorated house and most beautiful garden.

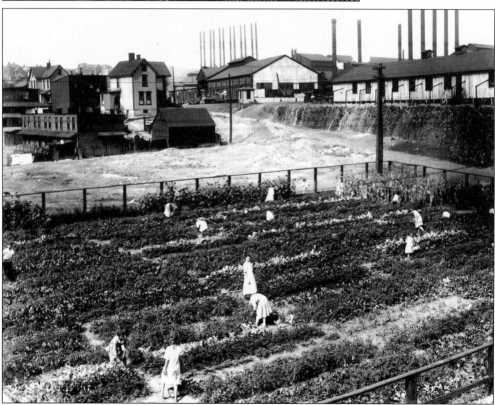

In addition to sponsoring the beautiful house contests, the Carnegie Steel Company also promoted vegetable and flower gardening for Duquesne's youth. Such programs benefited the community not only by teaching children how to work with their hands but also by turning empty dirt lots into fields of colorful flowers and food for the community.

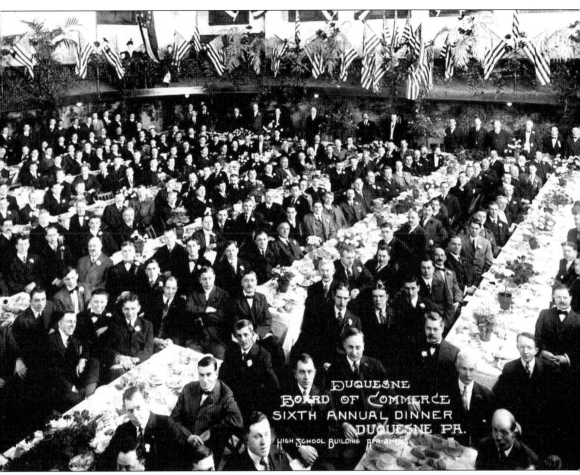

In this April 1915 photograph, the Duquesne Board of Commerce holds its sixth annual dinner in the high school gymnasium. In attendance were over 600 members of the Duquesne business and civic community. At the previous year's dinner, one of the guests of honor was Andrew Carnegie, who reportedly told a group of mill executives, "Buying the steel plant in Duquesne was one of the best investments I ever made."

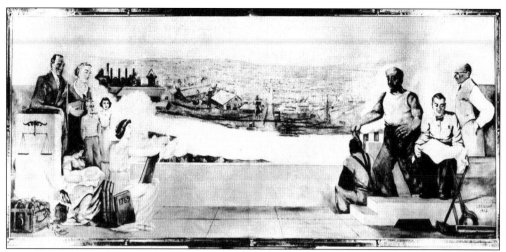

A painting by Levi Claggett called *Civic and Industrial Cooperation Promotes Prosperity* depicts the idea that communities and the industries that flourish within them need to work together. During his life, Claggett painted many beautiful works of art. An interesting fact is that Claggett had very large hands, and he seems to have passed this trait along to the subjects in his artwork, who often are depicted with disproportionately large hands.

Many of the homes in the area were heated with coal, and people were able to buy coal from the mill for use in their homes. The Carnegie Steel Company delivered coal in the community using a horse-drawn wagon. When customers made a coal purchase, they were given a receipt like the one shown here.

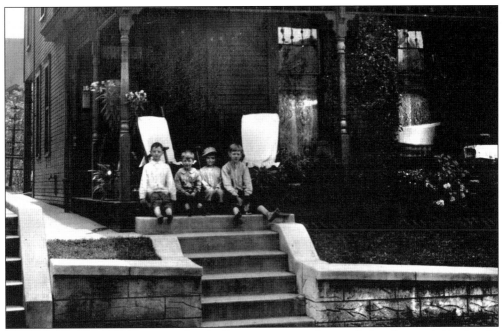

Known as a great place to raise a family, Duquesne was a cluster of close-knit neighborhoods. These four youngsters wait patiently for dad to come home from a hard day's work at the mill.

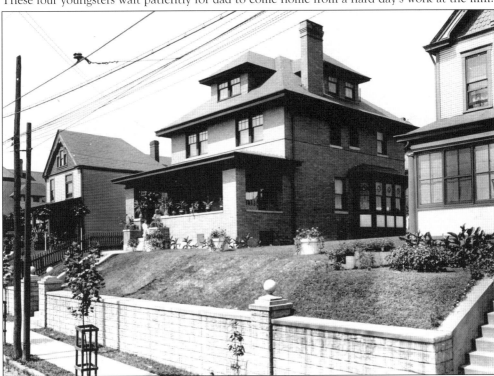

Quite a few of Duquesne's business owners lived in the two-story brick homes on Kennedy Avenue. The middle house looks pretty much the same today except for the sapling out front; the tree now stands 50 to 60 feet tall.

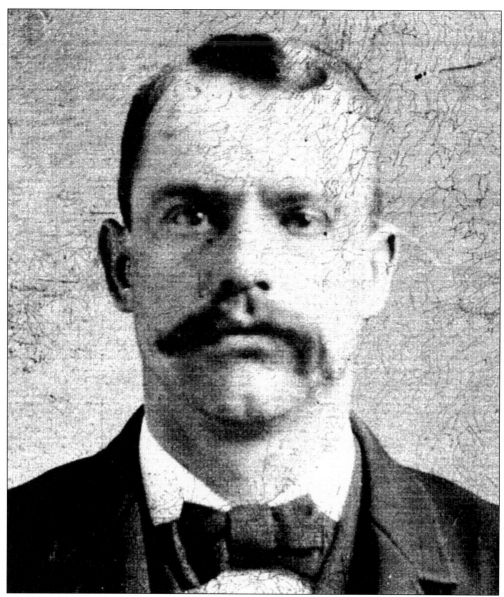

Max Raible arrived in Duquesne in 1874. He was born in Württemberg, Germany, in February 1862. As a Duquesne resident and businessman, he maintained a keen interest in the community and in the welfare and progress of the town and its residents. In the early days of the borough, he served as a council member. He was regarded as a good, level-headed man who had clear ideas for the future of the town. He enjoyed the respect and esteem of his neighbors and colleagues, and he was characterized in his *Duquesne Times* obituary as having an "inflexible integrity and honesty of purpose." He was known to be liberal and generous to a fault. At the time of his death in 1928, he was an active member of St. Joseph's Catholic Church, the Knights of Columbus, and various other civic organizations.

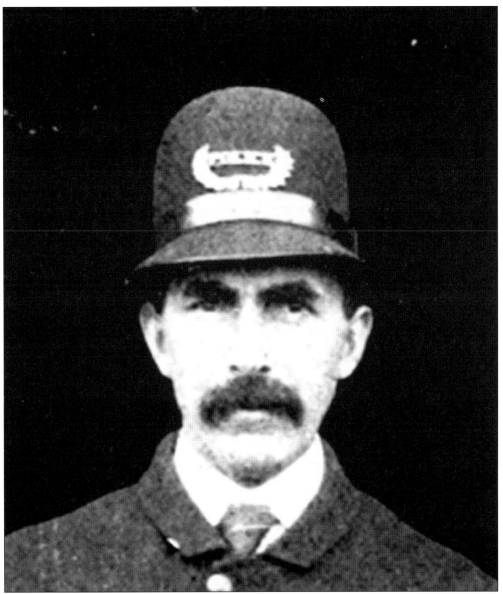

John "Jack" Gallagher was born in Charlestown, Ireland, in the county of Mayo on January 6, 1856. Immigrating to America in 1877, he worked in the coal mines until the steel industry arrived in the Mon Valley. Around 1900, he left his job in the Carnegie Steel mill and joined the Duquesne Police Department. His experience as a wrestler back in Ireland came in handy, and his size also played a factor in his success as a police officer: he stood over six feet tall and had a large build. He was a well-respected and honorable man. After serving as a police officer for more than a decade, Gallagher became constable of the Third Ward of the city, a position of great regard that he held for more than 20 years. He helped organize Holy Name Roman Catholic Church, and his signature can be found on the document that incorporated the city of Duquesne in 1892.

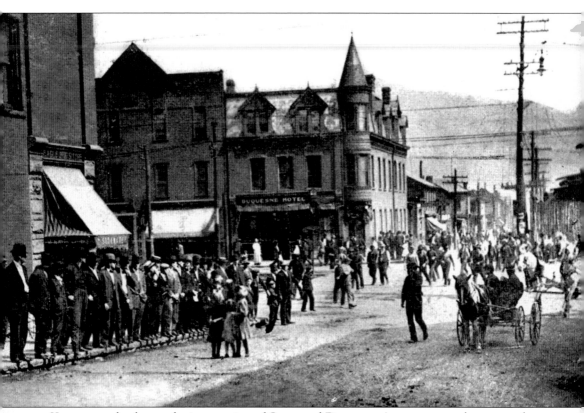

Known as a deathtrap, the intersection of Grant and Duquesne Avenues was a dangerous place to be, not just because of the traffic but also due to the characters who frequented the corners. A local newspaper described the situation: "[T]he use of intoxicants was very common. It was dangerous, especially for a foreigner, to appear about the First National Bank corner with a keg of beer on his shoulder. He was almost certain to be toppled over and relieved of his liquor."

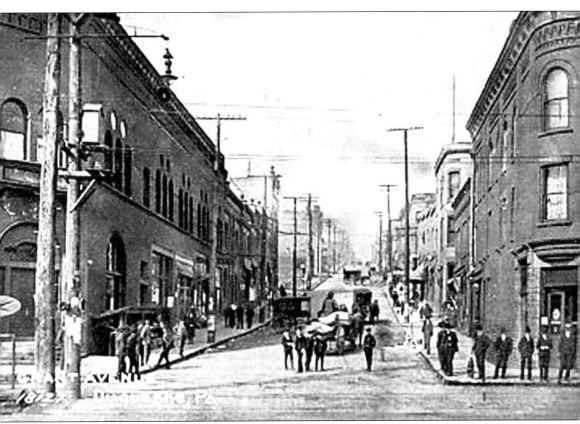

This view, looking west on Grant Avenue, shows one of the many dangers associated with the roadway. On more than one occasion, carts and wagons broke from their moorings and animal teams, and rolled to the bottom of the hill, injuring or killing anyone in their path.

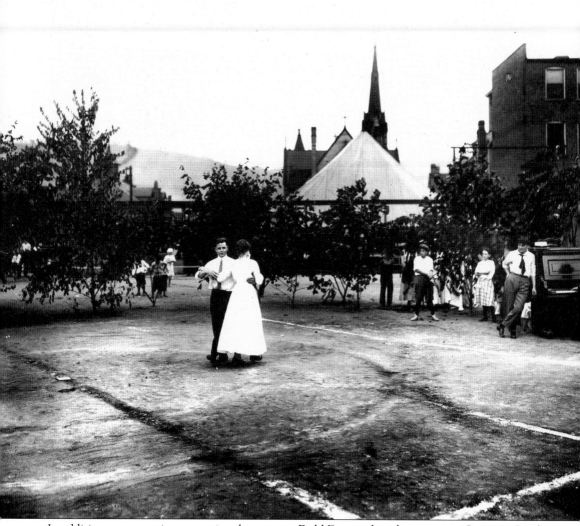

In addition to sponsoring recreational programs, Field Day, and garden contests, Carnegie Steel sent out its photography department to record and document community events. Pictured here, a couple competes in the Field Day dance contest, complete with a piano player.

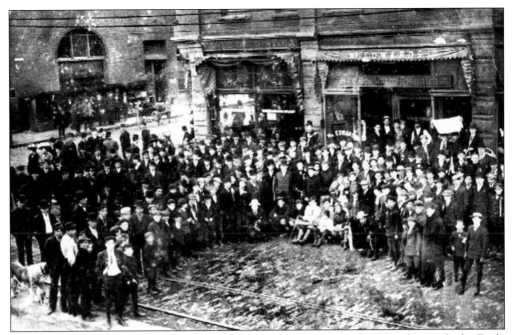

Numbering over 100 strong, the newsboys of Duquesne pose for a photograph outside the Eagle Drug Store. The *Duquesne Times*, the *Observer*, and the *Pittsburgh Sun Telegraph* were some of the publications they delivered to the many doorsteps of the town.

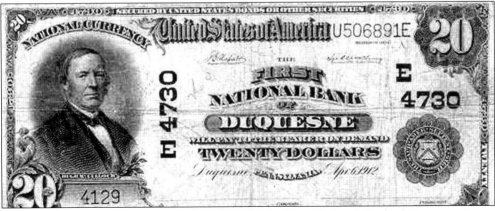

Shown here is a $20 note issued in April 1912 by the First National Bank of Duquesne. It was common for local banks to issue their own notes before the U.S. government standardized all paper money.

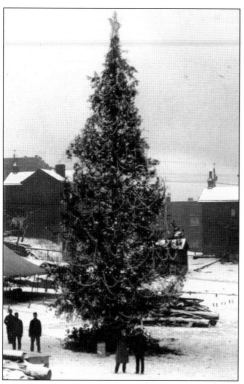

In 1912, Carnegie Steel erected a Christmas tree in front of the plant's general office. It was so well received that a year later mill superintendent Homer D. Williams presented Duquesne with its first Christmas tree. Erected in front of the library, the tree stood over 40 feet tall. The tradition was continued each year, with a Christmas tree set in front of city hall.

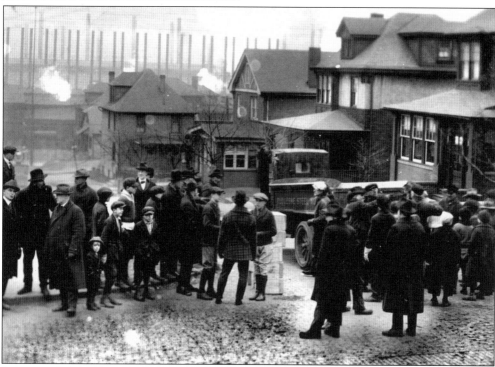

Because of their commitment to the town, workers of the Carnegie Steel Company could always be found at any of Duquesne's celebrations and gatherings.

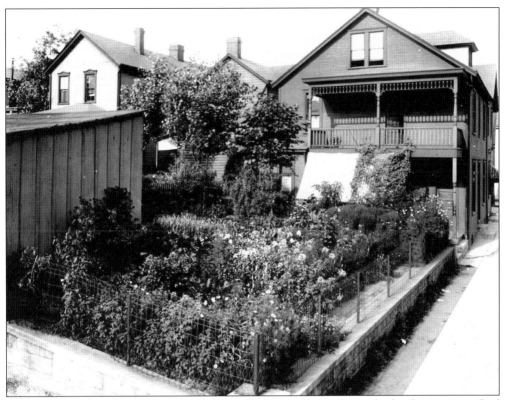

This garden at the corner of Fourth and Priscilla Streets shows the pride that homeowners had in their property and in their community. Shown here as a private residence, this building later became the Ken Park Hotel.

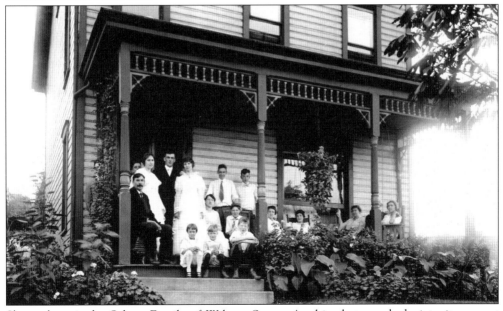

Shown here is the Schorr Family of Wilmot Street. As this photograph depicts, it was not uncommon for multiple generations and extended families to live under one roof.

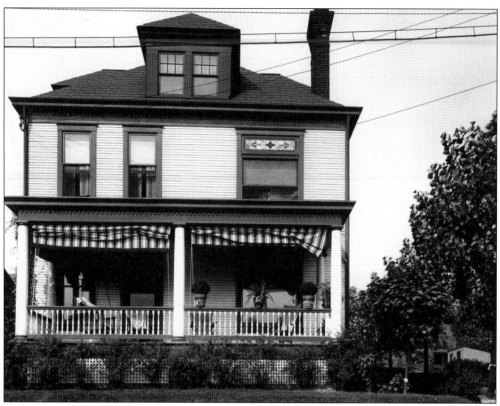

This two-story frame house, with its large front porch, stained-glass windows, and decorative trim, was a typical home in Duquesne. Each house was handcrafted and was built and maintained with pride.

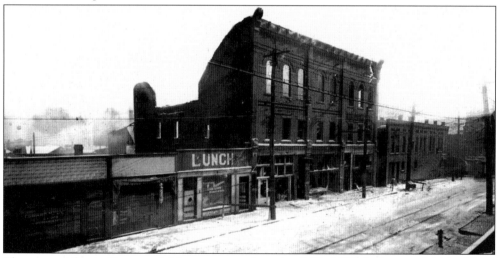

The greatest fire in Duquesne's history occurred on April 22, 1895. It destroyed 14 buildings and more than 25 businesses, including grocers, blacksmiths, feed and produce stores, dry goods merchants, and the town's post office. The origin of the fire was never determined, but damages were estimated at over $80,000. Duquesne's second-largest fire occurred just two months later, destroying 11 buildings.

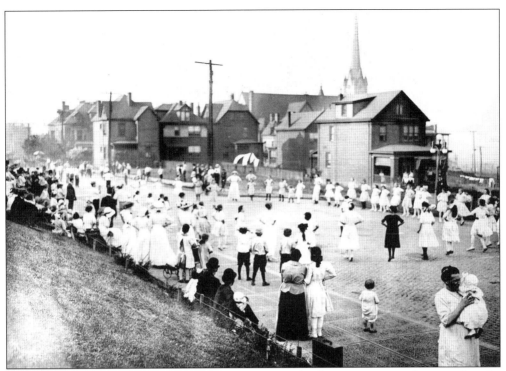

This photograph, taken in 1910, depicts a women's dance troupe performing for the community. Although the reason for the celebration is unknown, many of the townspeople seem to be enjoying the festivities.

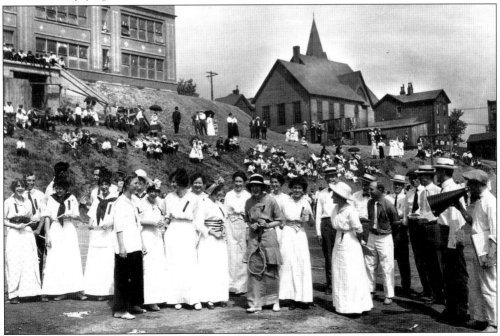

In the field behind city hall, a tennis exhibition begins with demonstrations and lessons by a local teacher.

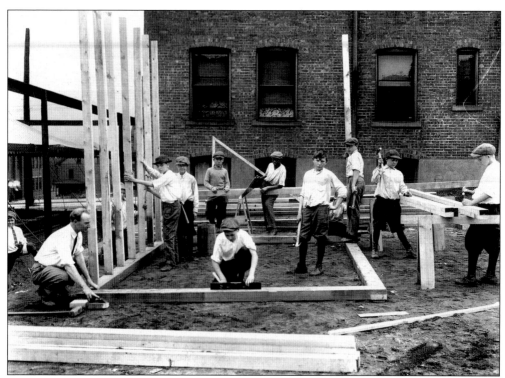

Before the Field Day festivities, young men from one of the local schools lend a hand in the construction of one of the many booths used in the festival. These booths housed games for the youngsters, as well as ethnic art and craft displays.

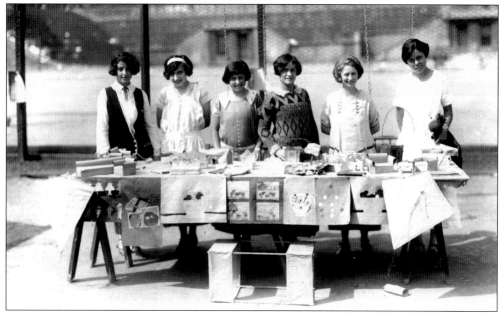

Six young ladies proudly show off their handmade arts and crafts such as chains, kites, and baskets, all made with various types of paper. The girls are in the playground beside city hall, 'in front of the high school.

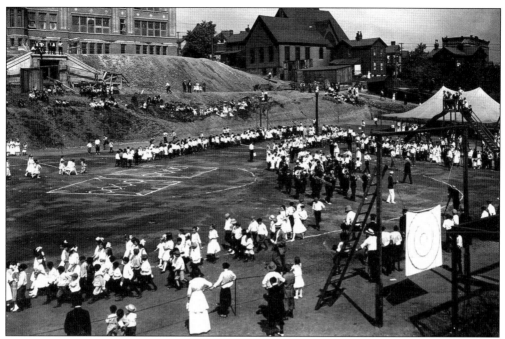

During a summer field festival, children march to the music of one of Duquesne's many bands. In the background is the old Methodist church and parsonage that were both eventually torn down to construct the war memorial.

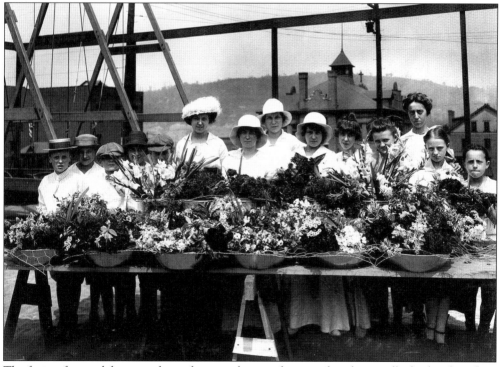

The fruits of many labors are shown here, as those with green thumbs proudly display their flora during yet another town celebration, Flower Day.

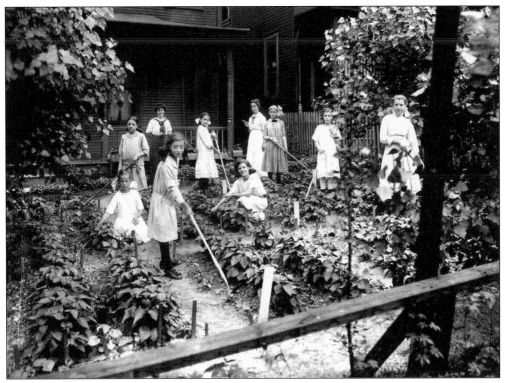

Neighbor helping neighbor was always the rule and not the exception. Schoolchildren were often seen cultivating the gardens of those less fortunate who were unable to tend their own crops.

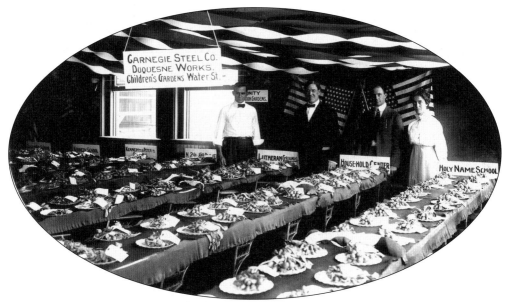

The various schools within the community were proud to show off what their students had grown. Among the schools represented here are Holy Name, House-Hold Center, Lutheran Grounds, North Second & Oliver, Kennedy, and Kennedy at Peter.

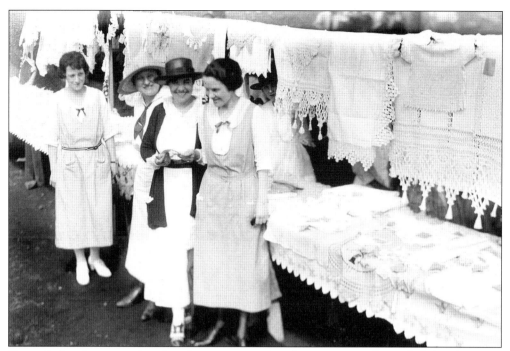

One of the demonstration booths at community festivities usually included a knitting, needlepoint, and crocheting display. Using skills handed down to them through many generations, these craftspeople demonstrate a level of expertise that is not often seen today.

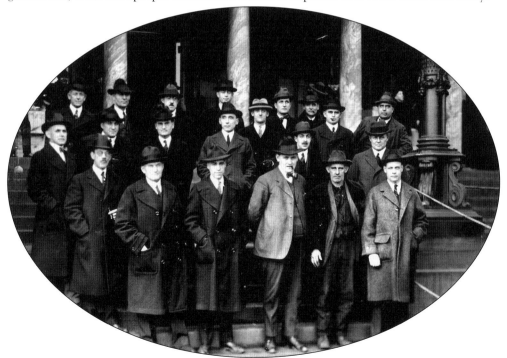

The executives and supervisors of Carnegie Steel's Duquesne Works pause after a meeting to pose for a group photograph outside the newly built library.

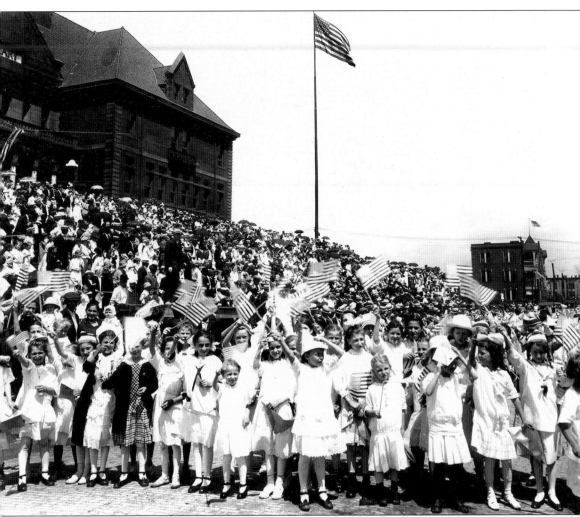

"They turned out as far as the eye can see!" That was how a local newspaper described the crowds at the 1914 Fourth of July parade. The function was dubbed Safe and Sane and featured games, dances, and contests for everyone. At the time this photograph was taken, the population of Duquesne was nearly 17,000; over 9,000 of those residents were children under the age of 10.

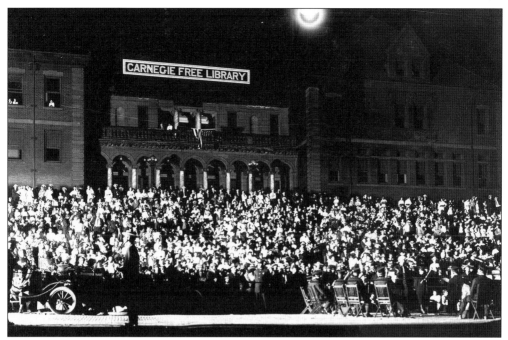

After a grand fireworks demonstration that capped off the Safe and Sane celebration, the townspeople were treated to a concert in front of the Carnegie Library. Those who were there agreed that the entire town was in attendance.

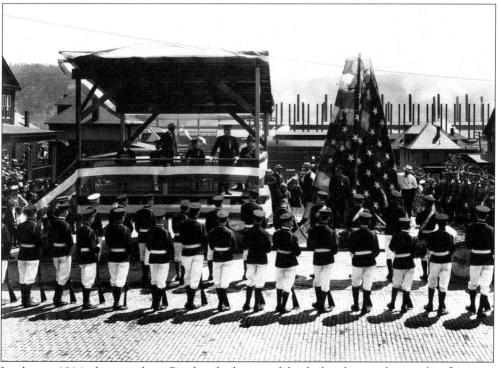

In this *c.* 1914 photograph, a Pittsburgh drum and bugle band, complete with rifle team, performs at the dedication of a new monument on Second Street at the top of Library Street.

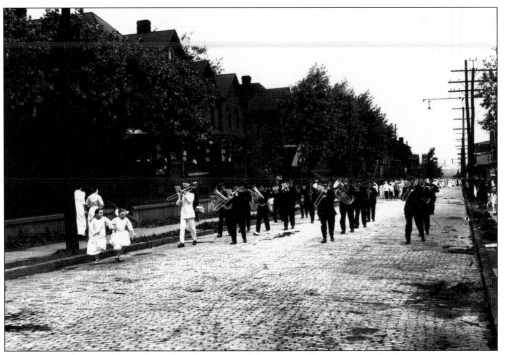

Children run to see a marching band performing in a parade on Kennedy Avenue.

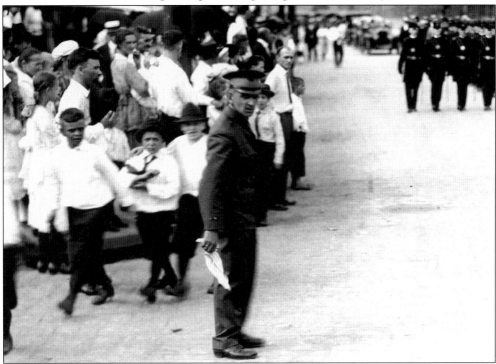

South Duquesne Avenue seemed to be the perfect place to hold a parade. The street was wide enough to accommodate the marchers, and there was plenty of room for onlookers on the side of the road.

Duquesne's Silver Jubilee, which commemorated the town's decree of incorporation, was a week-long event marked by parades, fireworks, dancing, and public celebrations. Duquesne's first 25 years saw the expansion of the mill, the construction of a new city hall and a new high school, and the completion of the streetcar lines linking the town with the newly annexed Duquesne Place and Kennywood Park.

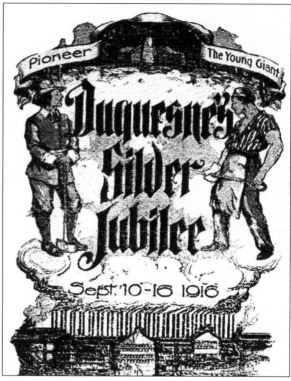

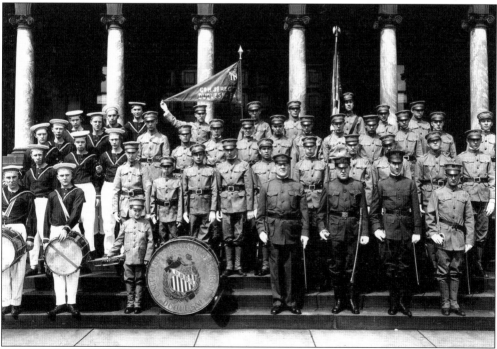

One of the many civic organizations in Duquesne was the United Boys Brigade 3rd Pennsylvania Regiment. This 43-man unit, complete with drum and bugle corps, performed at various town functions and celebrations.

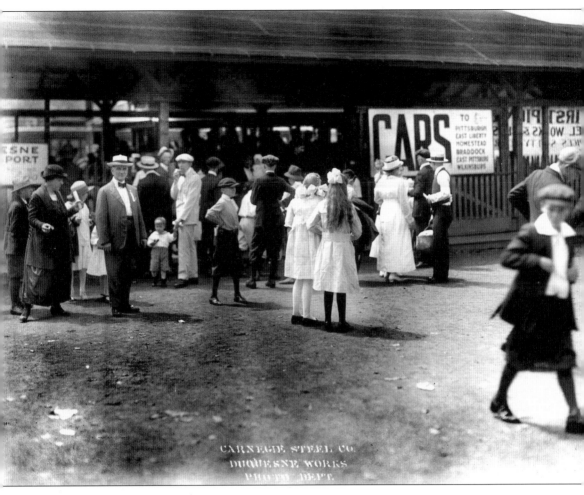

The first of many mill employee days at Kennywood was held in August 1920. This photograph captures the activity at the trolley station outside the park. Carnegie Steel Day featured activities, games, singing, and shows, all sponsored by the mill for its employees.

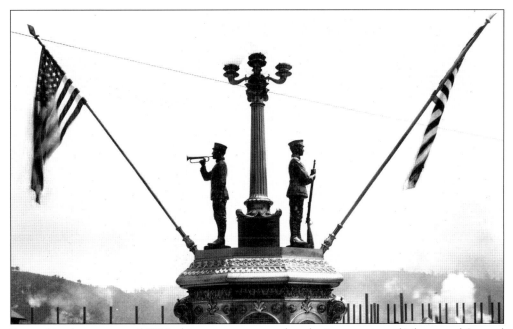

Erected in the summer of 1914, this monument stood at the intersection of Library and Second Streets. It was dedicated as a memorial to those who had fought in previous wars, and it bore as part of the inscription "as a lasting tribute." The statue was dismantled and melted down for a scrap metal contribution during World War II.

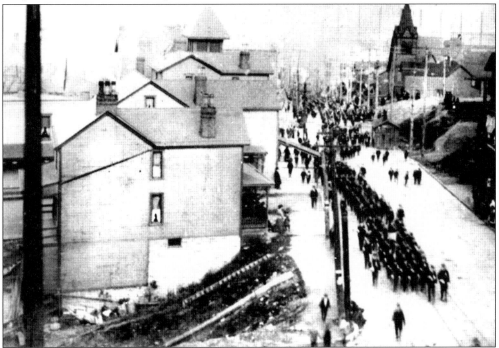

This *c.* 1910 photograph shows a rare glimpse of the top of Grant Avenue. The road was later widened to accommodate more traffic. Most of the houses seen on the left were torn down to make way for the expansion of businesses.

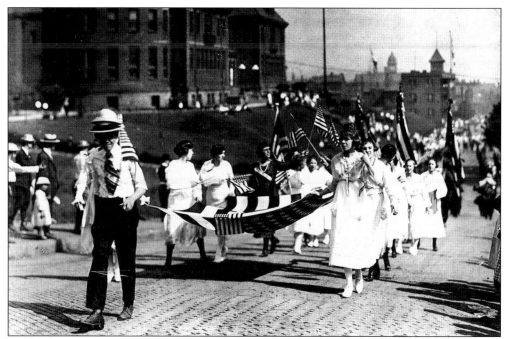

Although the Duquesne Women's Club was not officially organized until 1931, there were many women's groups that served in the community. Shown here is the Women's Temperance League marching past the library in one of the town's many parades.

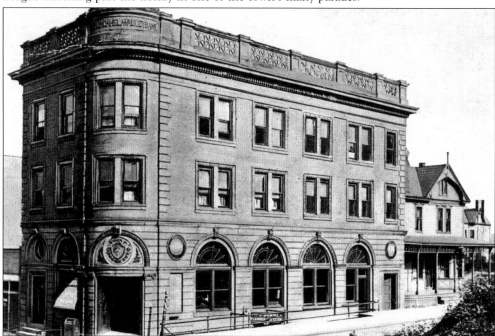

The first post office in Duquesne was established with the mills in 1886, but it burned down in the great fire of 1895. This building, at the corner of Second Street and Grant Avenue, served as the town's post office until a new building was constructed on South First Street. The new post office was dedicated in May 1938.

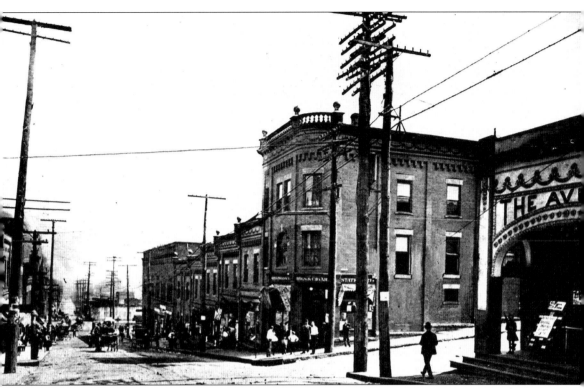

This view, looking down Grant Avenue at First Street, shows the Avenue News newsstand on the right. Years later, Avenue News became the Magic Lantern Theatre before becoming the Grand Theatre.

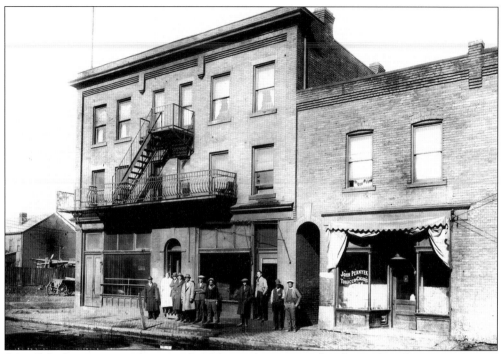

One of the businesses on the east side of the tracks was initially a bar and poolroom. By the end of 1920, there were 67 establishments within the town's limits that were licensed to sell liquor, either to patrons or wholesale.

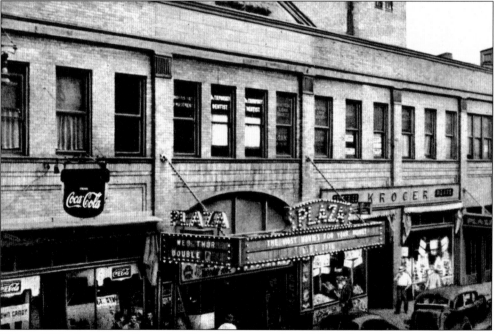

This *c.* 1940 photograph shows the Plaza Theatre on the old First Street. Once a major hub of business and activity, First Street was demolished in 1963 to make way for a commercial plaza. Among the businesses lost were the theater, Krogers, a drugstore, and dentists' and doctors' offices.

Four

THE LANDSCAPE

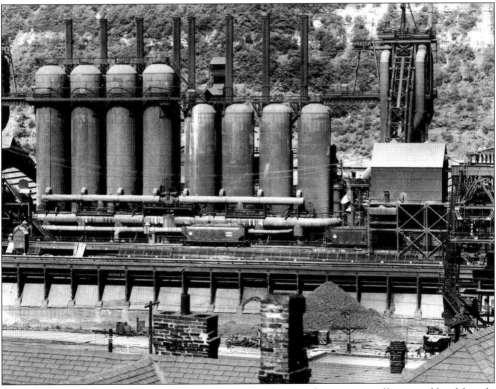

The Duquesne Steel Company began operations after purchasing a small tract of land beside the Monongahela River. The construction of what was to become a steelmaking giant changed the scenery of the town for the next 100 years. As the steelmaker continued to meet the demands of the expanding country, it needed to expand as well. In 1901, the mill consisted of 23 separate buildings; in 1925, that number jumped to 95 buildings, including all necessary power plants and administrative offices.

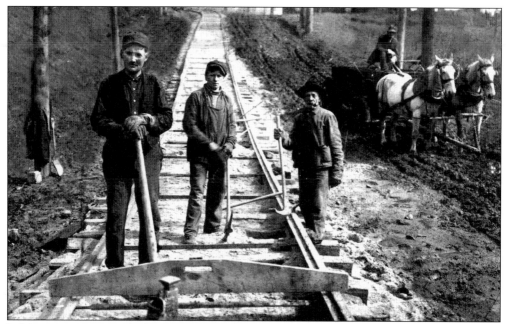

Laborers construct tracks for one of the few electric railways that operated in the area at the beginning of the 20th century. The first, the White Electric Traction Company of McKeesport, ran service from McKeesport to Cochran Station in Duquesne. This and other electric railways eventually linked Pittsburgh to towns as far away as Connellsville.

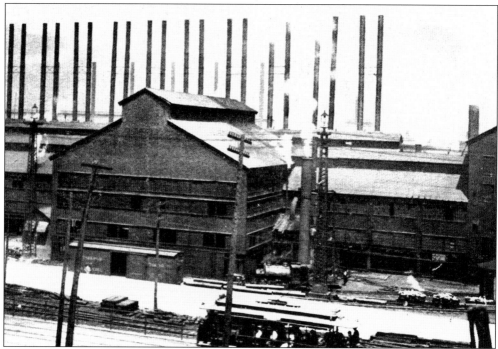

In 1889, the Braddock-Duquesne Street Car Company was granted permission to operate from the Huselton Farm (now Duquesne Place) to Grant Avenue via Duquesne Avenue. This rail line linked Duquesne to Kennywood Park.

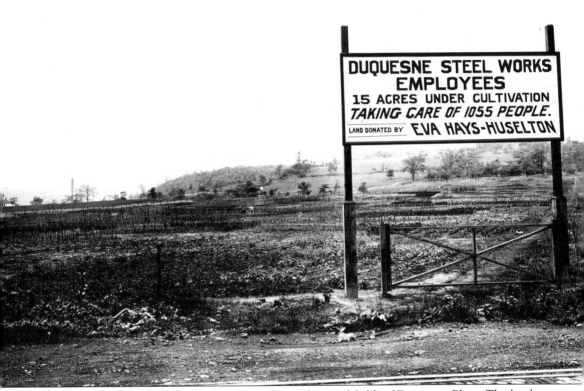

This 1915 photograph, looking west, shows the gardens and fields of Duquesne Place. The land was donated by Eva Huselton and maintained by the Duquesne Works of the Carnegie Steel Company. The land was used to teach people how to grow and cultivate crops. The vegetables grown here went to feed families in distress within the borough. The smokestack of the dump's incinerator can be seen in the left distance.

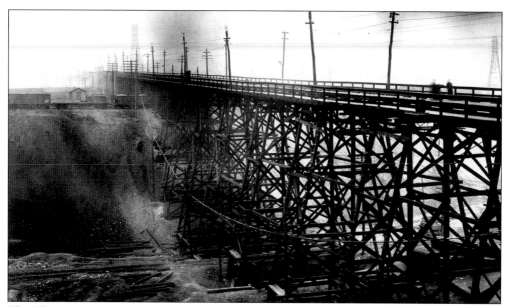

The Thompson Run Bridge was originally a wooden structure. Built in 1898, it carried horse-drawn wagons, foot traffic, and even streetcars to the area known today as Duquesne Place. The wooden span was eventually replaced by a permanent concrete structure, becoming what is the modern Route 837.

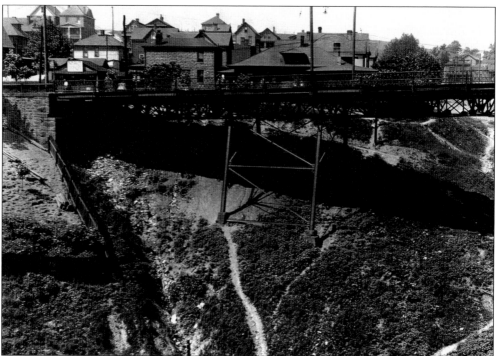

The Fifth Street Bridge spanned the gully between Priscilla Avenue and Cochran Street. The gully was a natural depression in the land that was not only deep but also prone to flooding because it sloped down to the Monongahela River. The gully was eventually filled in, and the few houses under the bridge and the bridge itself were buried.

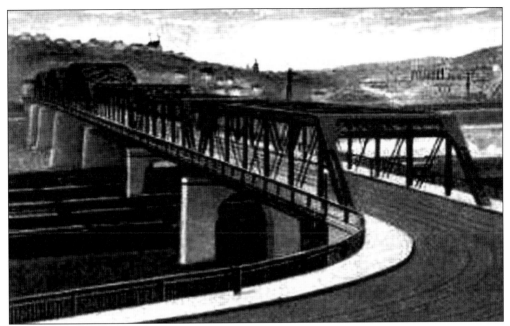

Built in 1891, the first Duquesne-McKeesport Bridge was the longest highway bridge in the state of Pennsylvania at the time of its construction. Prior to its erection, the only way to get to McKeesport from Duquesne was to cross the Monongahela by ferry or to traverse the river by foot when the ice was thick enough during the winter.

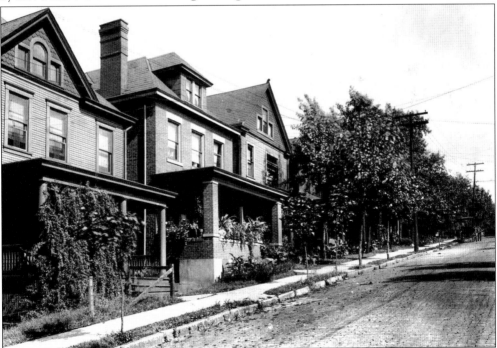

Looking south on Second Street from Hamilton Avenue, this photograph shows the residential houses that mainly constitute the north side of town. Many of the structures on the southern end of Second Street consisted of businesses and public buildings.

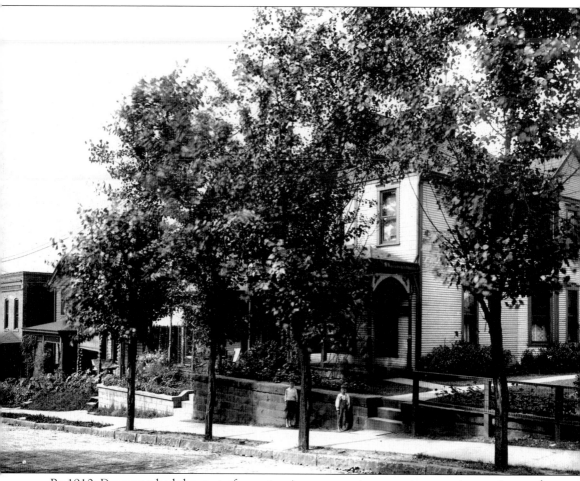

By 1910, Duquesne had the start of an extensive sewer system, a water-pumping station, and 18 miles of water mains running under the streets of the town. Many of the streets within the borough were paved with brick. Shown here is a house on North Fourth Street near Grant Avenue.

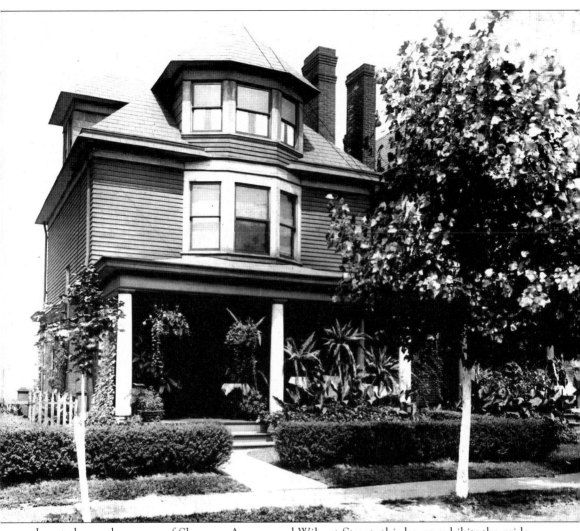

Located near the corner of Sherman Avenue and Wilmot Street, this house exhibits the pride taken by Duquesne homeowners in the maintenance of their property. The picture was taken by a Carnegie Steel Company photographer.

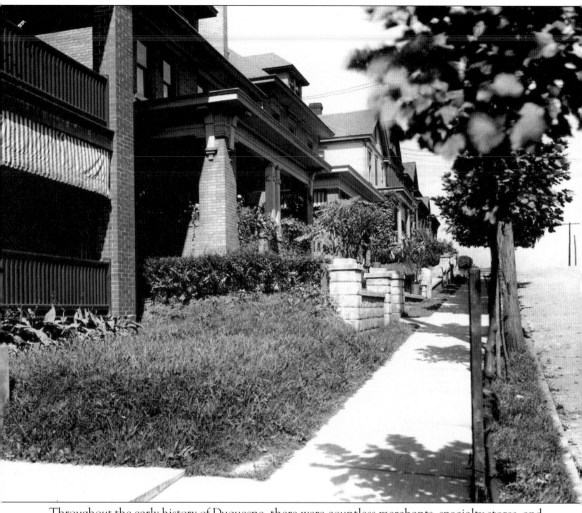

Throughout the early history of Duquesne, there were countless merchants, specialty stores, and shops located along the main streets of town. In addition, there were local delivery men, who were common sights on the streets as they brought their services door-to-door. Among them were butchers Max Raible and Gregor Manns and milkmen John Fey, John Walter, Sid Davis, and Nick Blank.

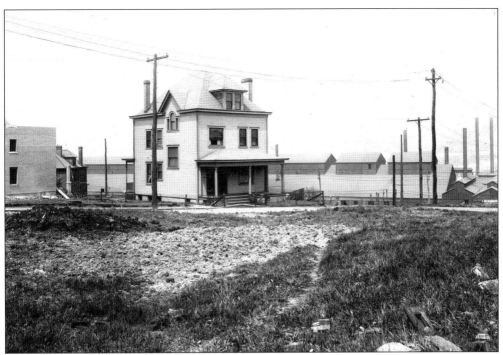

This house, located at the top of Second Street and Oliver Avenue, was one of the first built after 1900 in this area of town. As the mill continued to expand, so did the need for housing for its employees.

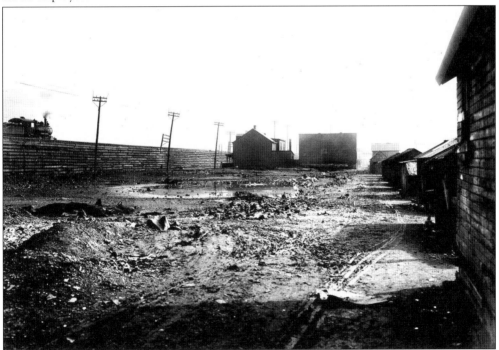

This photograph depicts the land below the tracks at Superior and Water Streets before the area was developed by the Carnegie Steel Company as a swimming pool and recreation area.

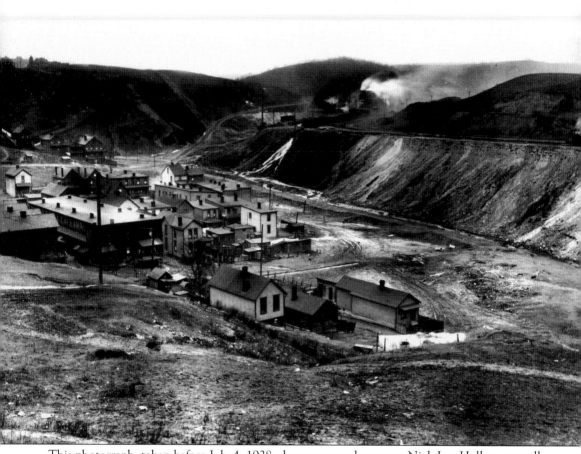

This photograph, taken before July 4, 1928, shows an area known as Nick Lee Hollow, a small community of a little over three dozen houses and a couple of multifamily tenements. The working-class families who lived here dwelled at the bottom of a trench made up of two decades of slag dumped from the mill. This slag came to make a depression in the land, forming a bowl-shaped landscape. Many of the families who lived in Nick Lee are known in the community today; their names include Oeler, Benda, Palyo, Stanczak, Petrisko, Mitchell, Punzak, Claggett, Jakubovics, Bornyak, Burda, Gedman, Brinsko, Gaca, Charak, Padakowski, Moses, Chalko, Kotzur, and Jackson.

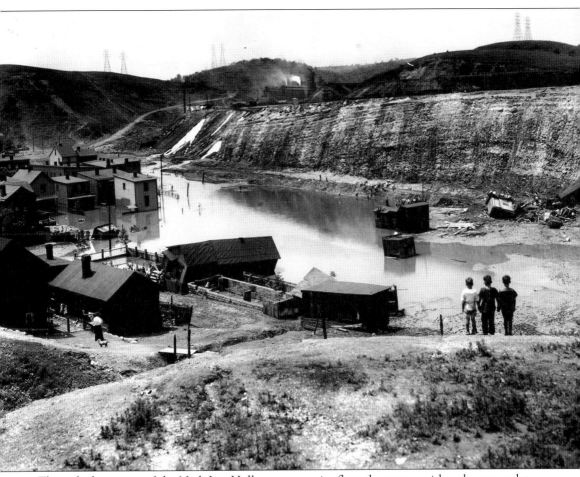

Through the center of the Nick Lee Hollow community flowed a stream with only one outlet, a small drainage pipe about four feet in diameter. On July 4, 1928, a horrific summer storm hit, bringing with it torrential rains. Debris carried by the stream quickly clogged the small drainage pipe. Soon the water began to rise, and within minutes the houses built to accommodate the mill workers and their families began to flood. Although there was no loss of life, the property loss was devastating. The homes in Nick Lee Hollow were never reclaimed, and the area was eventually filled in with slag. After the area was filled in, the land was used mainly by the Union Railroad, with a portion occupied by a scrap yard.

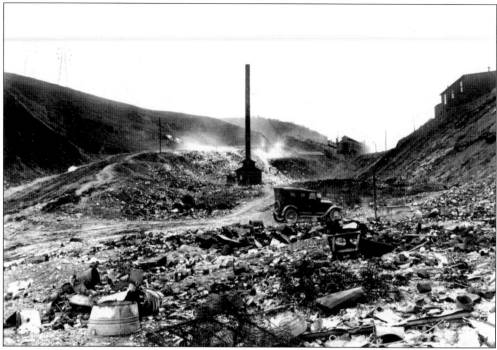

This image shows the Duquesne dump and incinerator, which were located just above Nick Lee Hollow. After the flood of July 4, 1928, the incinerator was relocated to the top of Polish Hill.

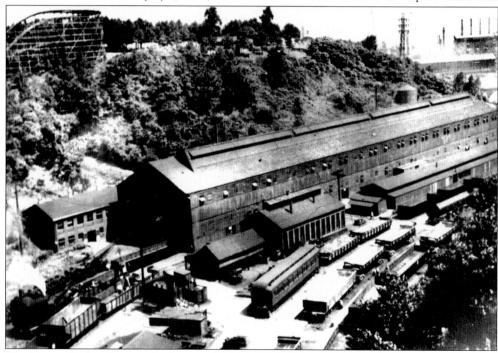

The Union Railroad repair facility was located in a hollow just below Kennywood Park. This *c.* 1920 photograph shows the repair yard, the Edgar Thomson Works in Braddock (upper right), and a Kennywood roller coaster (upper left).

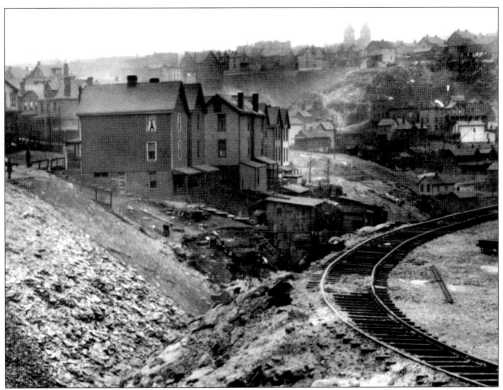

As the need for housing in Duquesne increased, available land became scarcer. This photograph shows structures crowded along the hillside of the Polish Hill area. The bell towers of St. Joseph's Church can be seen in the far distance.

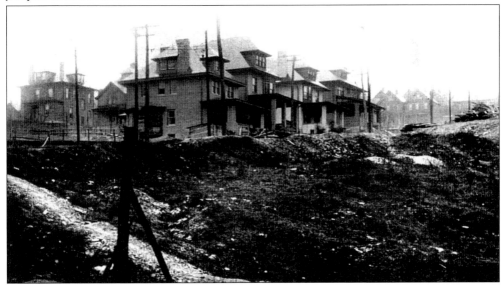

This c. 1910 photograph shows the four houses in the 300 block of Kennedy Avenue that were built to accommodate the mill superintendent and his managers. The property directly across the street from these houses was later renovated for the construction of the Duquesne High School.

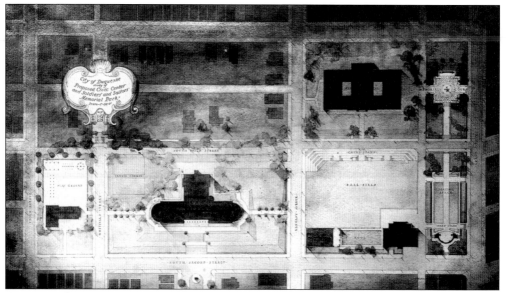

On November 11, 1921, Duquesne's Soldiers and Sailors Memorial Park was dedicated. The entire plot took up the approximate area of one-half of a city block; it had been scaled down from the initial plan (pictured), which called for nearly three city blocks.

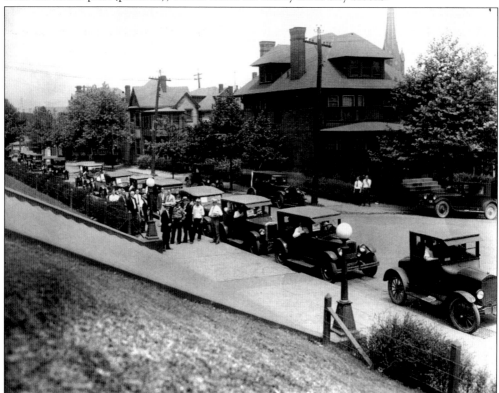

The Duquesne Library hosted many civic events, celebrations, and meetings. Among the rooms in the library that lent themselves to these gatherings were the reception room, two classrooms, and a lecture room.

One of the oldest and most recognizable landmarks in the city was the Duquesne City Bank. Established in 1903, it was originally known as the Duquesne Trust Company. The bank was built at the corner of First Street and Grant Avenue. Although it was remodeled in 1917, the bank stayed in the same location until the razing of the businesses in that block for the construction of a new shopping plaza in 1963. Shown here c. 1930 are the bank executives under the landmark clock.

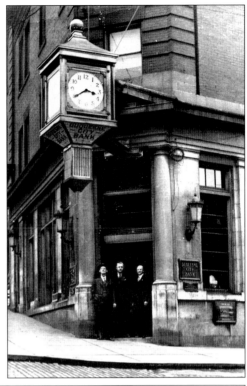

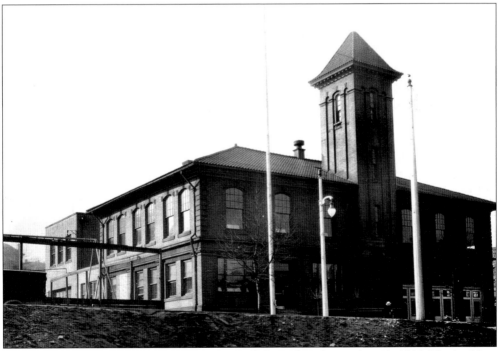

The new city hall on South Second Street was dedicated on September 10, 1912. The building contained the borough offices, chambers for borough council meetings, police station, jail, and fire department.

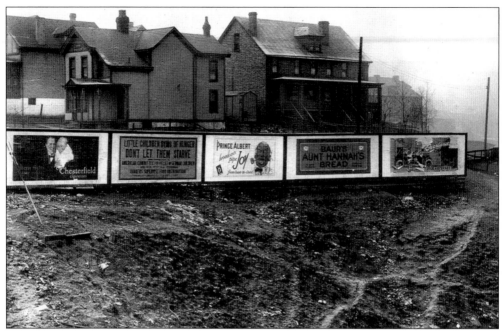

Advertisers take advantage of the hillside just above the heavily traveled Thompson Run Bridge to market their product to those entering Duquesne by cart, foot, or trolley.

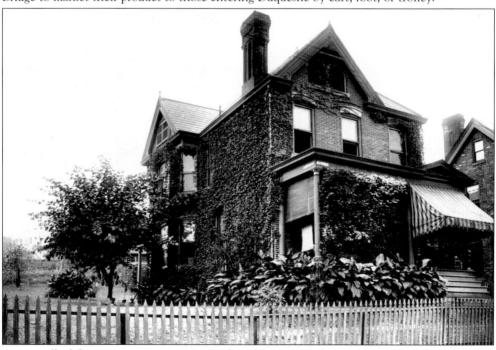

Among all of the growing communities within the Monongahela River Valley, Duquesne was often credited as being the most progressive in government and overall city maintenance. From Duquesne's inception, the town fathers recognized the need to keep resources and services in line with the town's continuing growth. These services included street maintenance and water and sewer services.

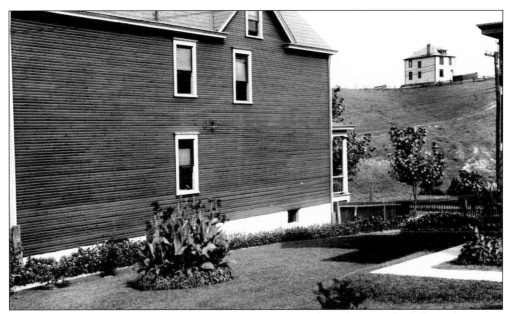

Looking toward Crawford Avenue from Savey Street, this photograph depicts the sparse population in the Third Ward c. 1913. Within two decades, what is seen here as farmland was sold and developed for residential houses.

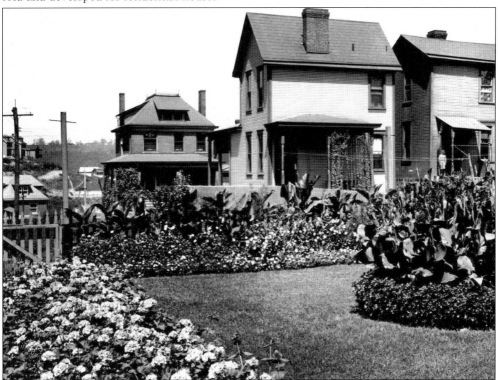

In addition to maintaining beautifully landscaped yards, German immigrants also brought the tradition of growing hops to Duquesne. The hops vines grew along strings, as seen on the rear porch in this photograph.

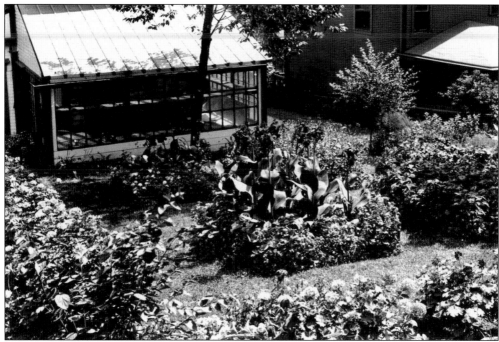

Black-and-white photographs do not do justice to the beautifully landscaped yards consisting of bright-colored flowers and a wide variety of tropical plants, including cannas and elephant ears.

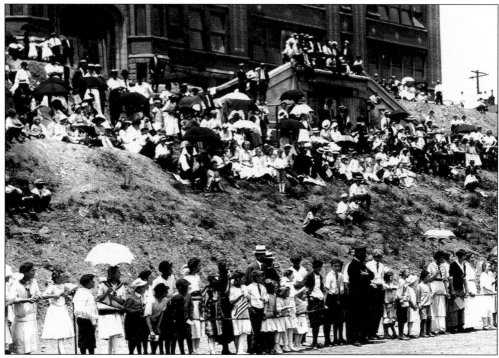

Although many of the town's festivities and celebrations were held throughout the community, some were coordinated in the field between city hall and the high school. Shown here are dozens of residents, some with picnic baskets in hand, enjoying the activities on a warm summer day.

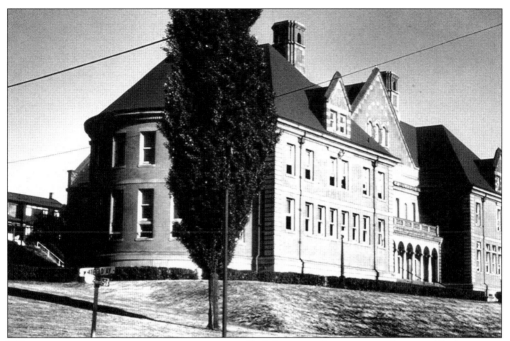

Whenever a community activity or event called for an indoor venue, the possible locations included the various church halls, the high school gymnasium, Turner Hall, or the library's music hall or reception room.

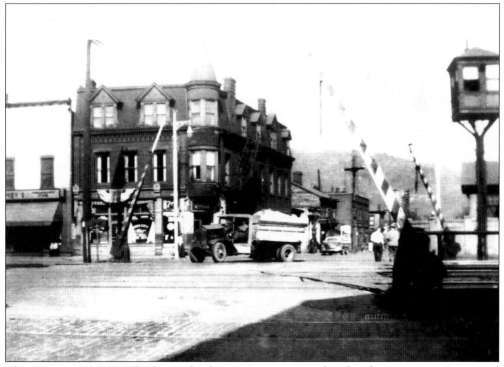

This *c.* 1940 photograph shows the busy intersection and railroad crossing at Grant and Duquesne Avenues.

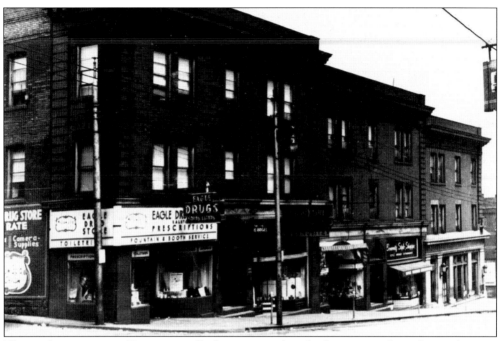

Those who grew up in Duquesne will always remember the businesses along Grant Avenue, including the Eagle Drug Store (complete with its soda fountain), Benovitz Refrigeration, Book's Shoe Store, and Benovitz Style Shoppe.

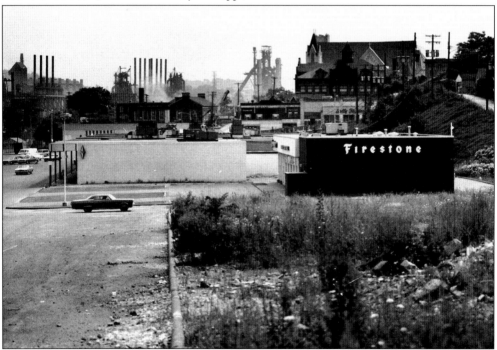

The late 1960s saw dramatic changes to the landscape in the First Ward. Although in this photograph the mill looms yet unchanged in the background, the Duquesne Shopping Plaza stands where the old First Street businesses once existed.

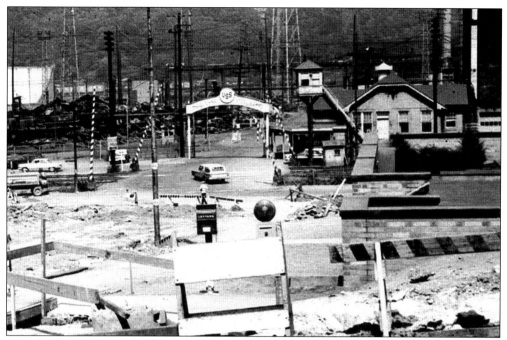

Part of the continuing change in the First Ward was the redesign and construction of the intersection of Grant Avenue and Route 837 (Duquesne Avenue). On the right of the photograph can be seen new construction where the First National Bank of Duquesne once stood.

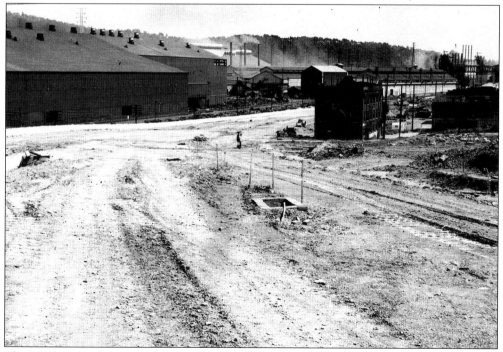

The 1960s redevelopment program also included replacing the old Duquesne Avenue with a four-lane interstate highway. Most of the buildings had to be demolished to make way for this expansive roadway, as shown here.

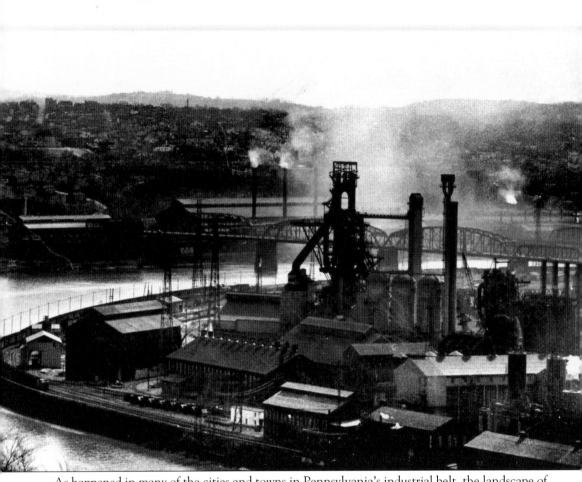

As happened in many of the cities and towns in Pennsylvania's industrial belt, the landscape of Duquesne was forever changed when the mills closed, not only by the absence of the huge steelmaking monsters but also by the lack of haze that had spewed from their stacks. It was industrial towns like Duquesne that helped contribute to the title Pittsburgh was once given: the Smoky City.

Five
THOSE WHO SERVED

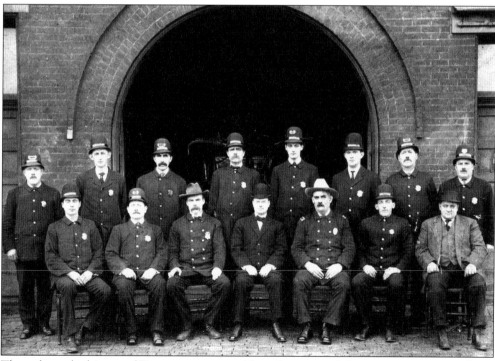

Throughout the history of Duquesne, many residents have served their country in times of war, often sacrificing their lives. Others dedicated themselves to serving their neighbors as police officers and firefighters. Until the borough's incorporation in the fall of 1891, the surety of the peace was mainly in the hands of vigilante patrols. These patrols roamed the town, enforcing local laws and keeping the citizenry safe. Those who made up the all-volunteer vigilante corps were familiar to the townspeople; they included Max Raible, John Lutz, William Thompson, and Tim Oldham. Pictured here is the police force in 1909.

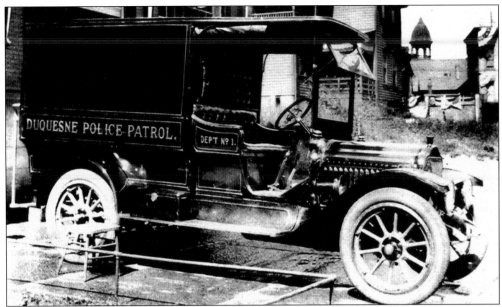

Shortly after its official formation, the Duquesne Volunteer Fire Department assembled its own band. Composed of fire department members, the band played at various civic functions and celebrations, such as the dedications of the library and the war memorial.

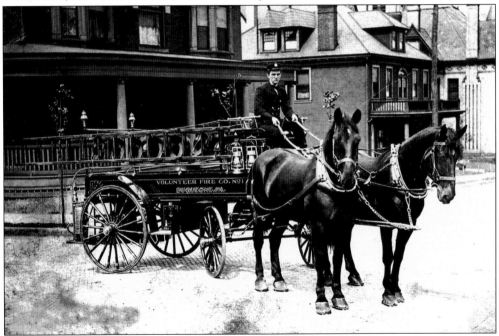

In the late 1870s, there were three volunteer fire stations in the community: Central, Germantown, and Dutchtown. Duquesne's first organized fire department was established in 1912. It consisted of a horse-drawn mini-pumper, a small ladder wagon, and two dozen men working two shifts each. Most of the water supplied to fight fires came from the town's fire hydrants, which were installed shortly after the fires of 1895. Here, the ladder wagon is drawn by the department's draft horses, Tommy and Chief.

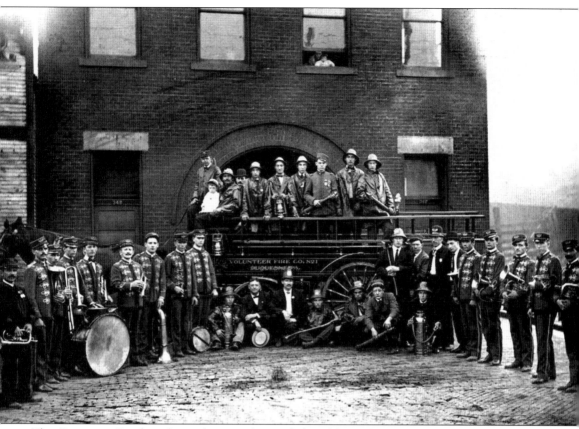

The Duquesne Band is shown here in front of the old city hall and firehouse on South Duquesne Avenue. The band played at all of the town events and celebrations, such as the dedications of the war memorial, city hall, and the Carnegie Library. Established in the 1890s, the band continued to entertain through the 1940s.

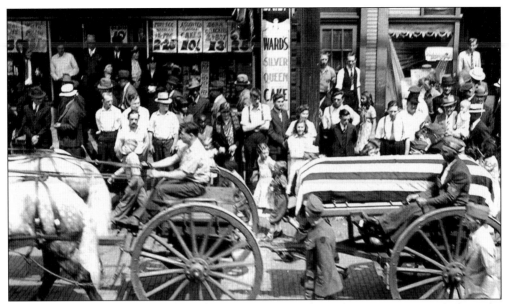

William Husak, a soldier killed in World War I, is honored by residents gathered along the sides of Grant Avenue on a sunny Sunday morning, as his coffin makes its way to its final resting place.

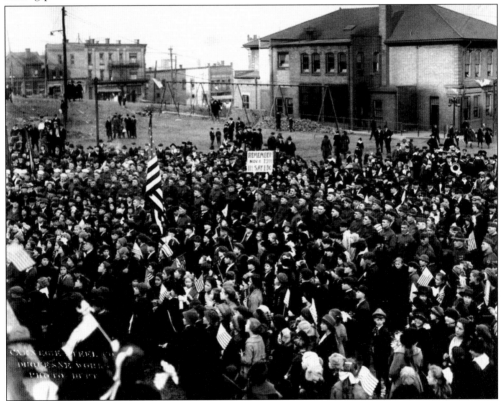

Hundreds of residents and soldiers gather in the field behind city hall in commemoration of Armistice Day in 1918, marking the end of World War I.

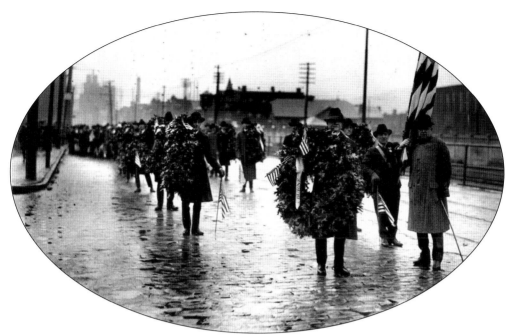

This photograph, taken on Duquesne Avenue, depicts the parade procession that wound through the city commemorating the dedication of the World War I monument. Shown here are men carrying wreaths bearing the names of those soldiers from Duquesne who fought and died in the war. The first wreath denotes the name of Raymond Burns, for whom the Veterans of Foreign Wars Duquesne Post is named.

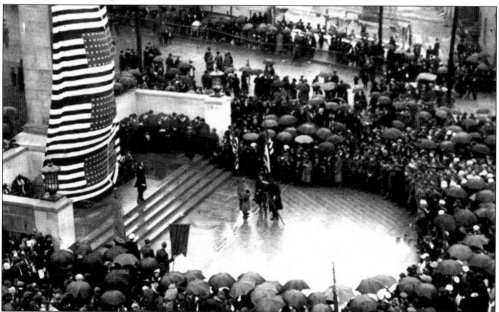

On a cold November day in 1921, over 3,000 residents, dignitaries, and military leaders turned out for the dedication of the World War I memorial. The somber occasion was marked by a parade featuring auxiliary military units and bands from Duquesne, as well as from surrounding communities.

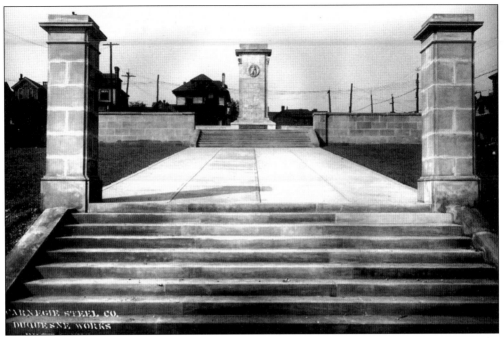

The World War I monument was a stone-and-bronze structure displaying the names of the town's 23 fallen sons. It stood at Grant Avenue and South Fourth Street until it was moved in the late 1990s to the park next to city hall.

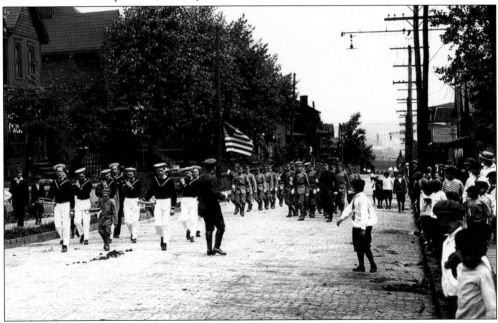

It is not widely known that Duquesne had its own company of volunteers during the American Civil War. The unit, organized by Byron Cochran, practiced and drilled every night of the week on the property now occupied by St. Joseph's Church. Among the volunteers in this unit were familiar names such as Goldstrohm, Carr, Stein, McClure, Doney, Bickerton, Thompson, Oskin, and Walker. Pictured here, local members of a military regiment march in a parade.

Six
READING, WRITING, AND RELIGION

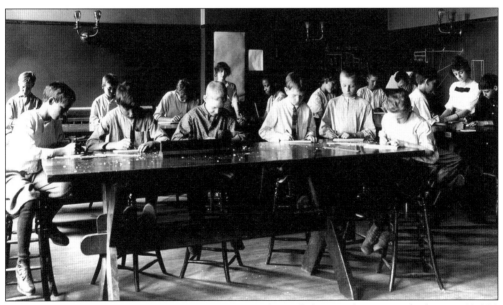

The census data for the city of Duquesne in 1920 showed the population at a little over 19,000 residents. The population of children under the age of 19 numbered slightly more than 8,700, with 42 percent of the children of foreign birth and 12 percent classified as illiterate. Through programs sponsored by Carnegie Steel and its employees, the Duquesne school system, and various community initiatives, these children were taught the basic skills of reading, writing, and arithmetic and were instructed in trades such as carpentry, masonry, advanced mathematics, and building construction. These skills were used not only for the expansion of the nation but also in the growth of this community.

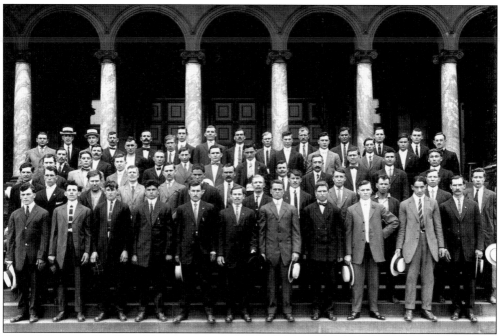

One of Carnegie Steel's welfare programs introduced foreign workers into American industry. This was accomplished by educating immigrants in reading and writing the English language. Shown here are the graduates of the 1914 class.

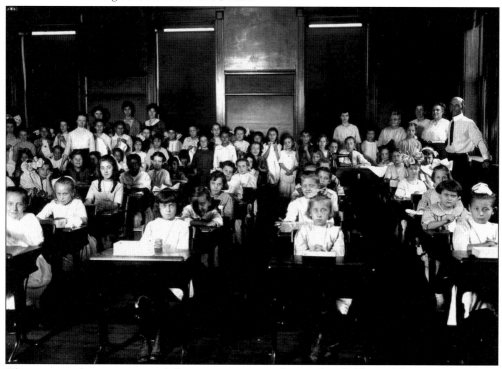

Classes were also set up around the community to educate the children of foreign immigrants in the ways of American life. Pictured here is a sewing class c. 1913.

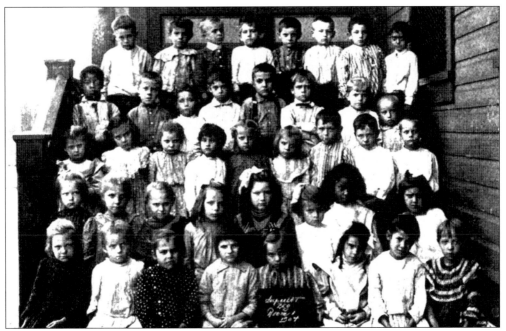

Pictured here is the Superior School class of 1904. These were the children of families who lived in and around Superior and Water Streets, the area known as "below the tracks."

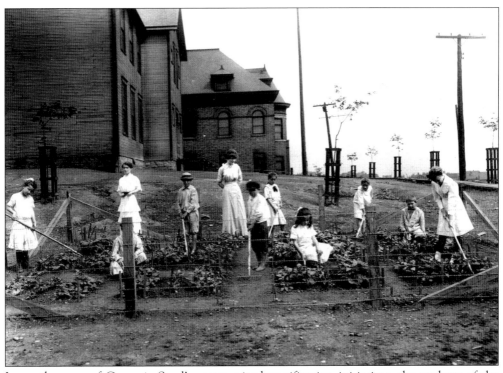

In another one of Carnegie Steel's community beautification initiatives, the students of the Oliver School, pictured here, turned what once was a dirt lot into a beautiful garden.

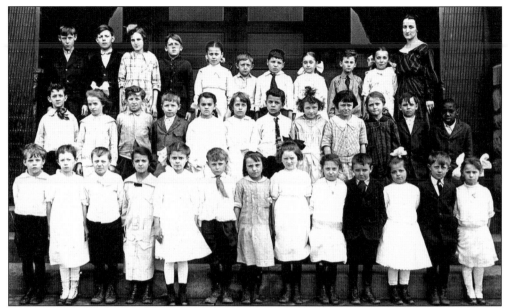

One of the many school buildings within Duquesne was the Crawford School, located at Crawford Avenue and Hill Street, pictured here in 1916. The first Crawford building was a four-room frame schoolhouse erected in 1889. In 1899, an eight-room brick building was constructed to accommodate more students. The school was torn down and replaced by the John F. Kennedy School, which has since been closed by the district.

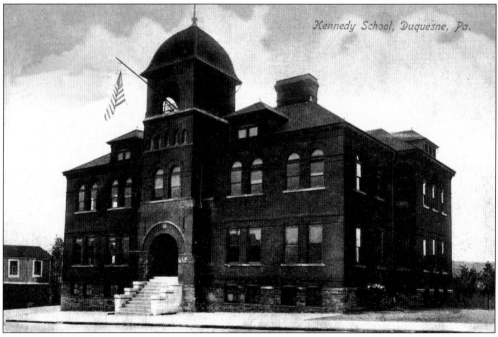

Pictured here is the Kennedy School, which was located on Sixth Street near Kennedy Avenue. The first Kennedy School building, erected in 1892, consisted of eight rooms. A four-room addition was built in 1898. The attendees of Duquesne schools came from all walks of life. Some of their parents were hourly mill workers; others were business owners and civic leaders.

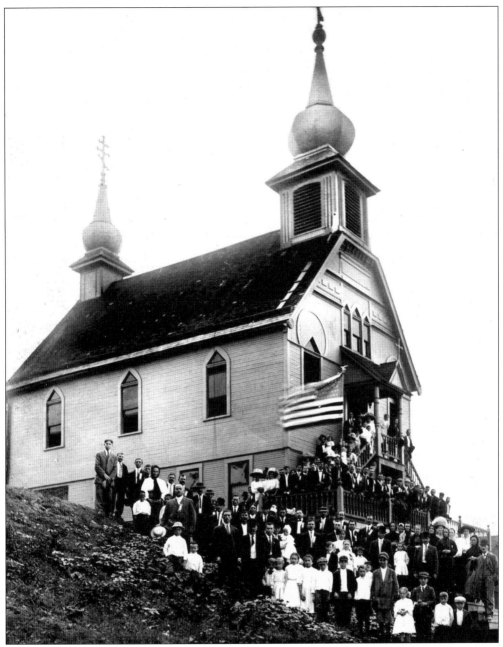

The St. Nicholas Greek Catholic Orthodox Church was organized in May 1891 with over 100 families. Shortly after the turn of the century, St. Nicholas saw over 200 families in attendance, not only from Duquesne but also from McKeesport and West Mifflin. The original wooden structure was located on Oak Street overlooking the Monongahela River. It was the second Greek Catholic Church established in America and the first in western Pennsylvania.

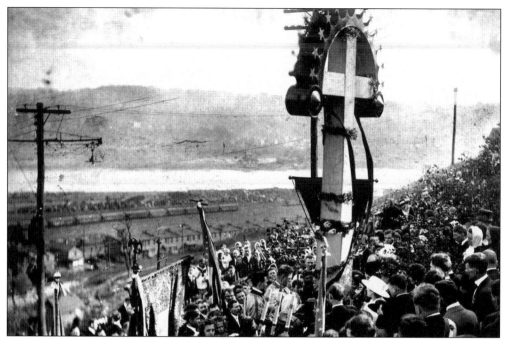

The religious creeds in Duquesne were as diverse as the town's many residents. In 1902, there were 16 churches in the city representing a variety of denominations, including Methodist, Presbyterian, Lutheran, Baptist, and Episcopal. There were 5 churches of the Catholic faith.

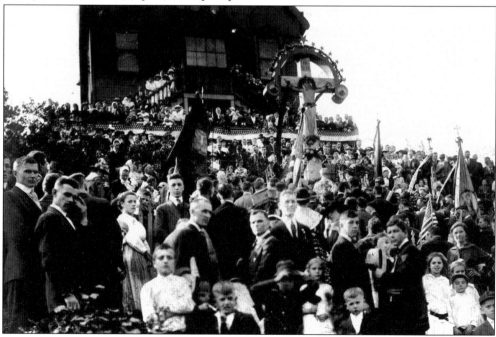

The beginning of the 20th century saw Duquesne as a bustling and sometimes turbulent town. Yet every Sunday the rush of activity slowed as the town's residents paused to worship. Businesses were closed as families, dressed in their best attire, met with their neighbors to praise and give thanks for what they had.

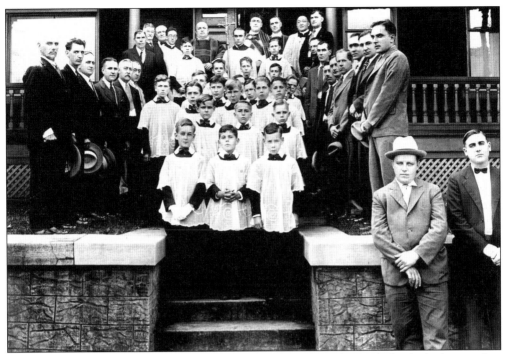

Serving as an altar boy in the church is a proud tradition in the Catholic faith that is often handed down through males in the family. Pictured here are the altar boys of St. Joseph's Church, standing in front of the old Grant Avenue parish house.

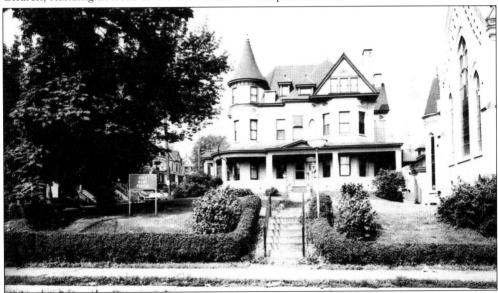

Holy Name Church was first organized in 1890, with the first services conducted over a store on Second Street. In July 1899, the cornerstone for the present-day church building was laid at the corner of Kennedy Avenue and First Street. With a seating capacity of 800, the church was dubbed the finest of its day. The total construction cost was about $50,000. Holy Name also boasts a magnificent pipe organ donated by Andrew Carnegie and installed in February 1901 at a cost of $6,000.

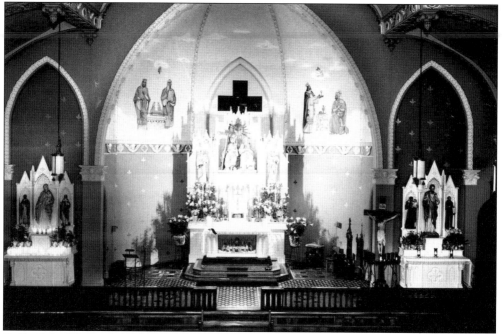

Sadly, few of the original churches established in Duquesne in the early part of the last century still stand. Those that are left include Holy Name (shown here), St. Joseph, St. Nicholas, and the First Presbyterian Church.

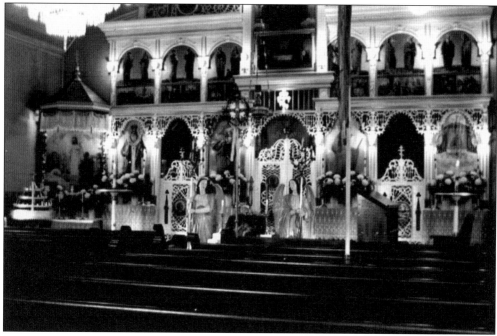

Established in 1902, Holy Trinity Church was erected on South First Street. Construction on the church was completed in 1905, but not without controversy. Rev. Nicholas Hodobay, the congregation's pastor, objected to the construction of a new church. After battles with the court and the bishop, the pastor was overruled. The church was completed, and the pastor resigned.

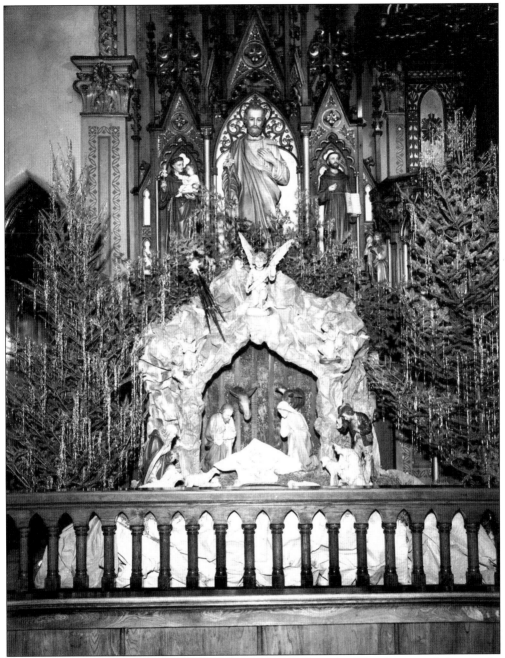

Christmas in Duquesne was truly a time of celebration and worship. Families attended midnight Masses and congregational celebrations marking the birth of a saviour. Pictured here is the creche in Holy Trinity Church *c.* 1940.

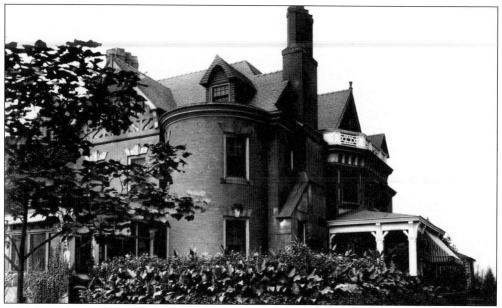

First formed in 1888, the First Presbyterian Church of Duquesne was organized with a membership of only 33. Its first building, located at the corner of Viola and Second Streets, was built at a cost of $23,000 and was dedicated in May 1894. After the church moved to its current location, at Route 837 and Fairmont Street, the old church was torn down to make way for residential development.

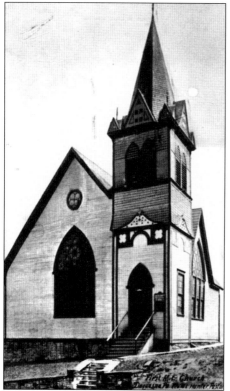

The African Methodist Episcopal Church, now known as Payne Chapel, was established in 1901. It was initially located in a small building at Seventh Street near Kennedy Avenue. A newer and larger building (shown here) was erected on that site in 1906.

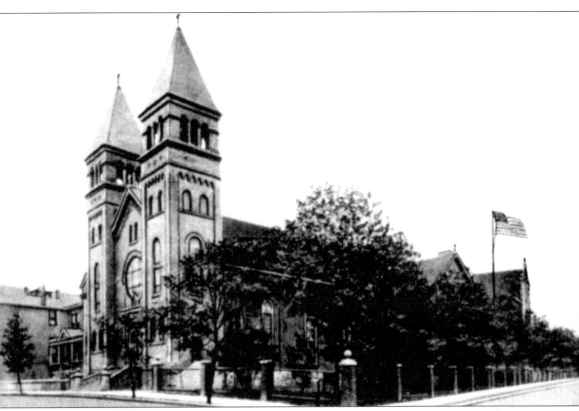

In 1895, prominent German Catholics Peter Stinner, Melchior Wolf, Joseph Mayer, and Peter Zewe together purchased property located at the corner of Grant Avenue and Auriles Street from the school district. St. Joseph's Church of Duquesne was formed after the construction of the building in 1898.

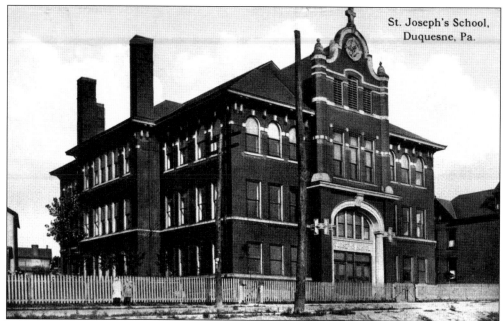

Soon after the construction of the church, St. Joseph's School was built. In 1902, the school had an enrollment of 70 pupils. By 1913, St. Joseph's was one of 15 school buildings, both public and parochial, located within Duquesne.

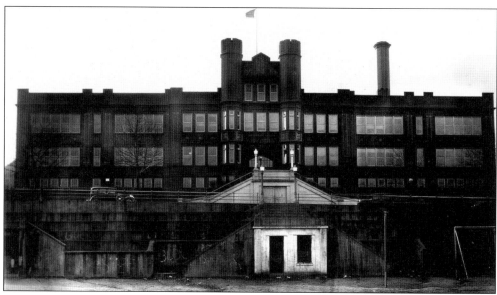

This c. 1930 photograph shows the Duquesne High School, which was constructed in 1913. It consisted of 33 rooms, an auditorium, and a gymnasium. Remodeled in the late 1990s, the building now houses all of the students from kindergarten through 12th grade in the Duquesne City School District.

Seven

JUST FOR FUN

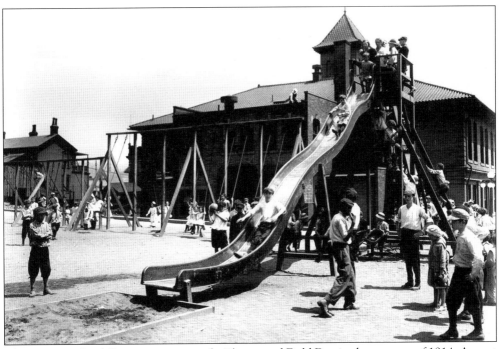

The Carnegie Steel Company sponsored a Playground Field Day in the summer of 1914. As part of the community recreation program it had initiated a year earlier, the company built playgrounds, ball fields, and a swimming pool for the children of Duquesne. The Second Street playground consisted of swings, slides, a ball field, sandboxes, and craft tables. Such events also featured exhibitions of quilting, knitting, and gardening.

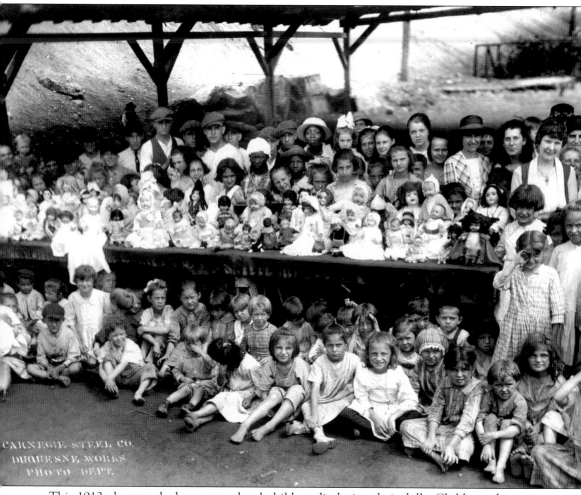

This 1912 photograph shows some local children displaying their dolls. Children who come from families of means, whose dolls are made of porcelain and are well-dressed, stand beside children from poor immigrant families, whose dolls are tattered and handstitched with yarn.

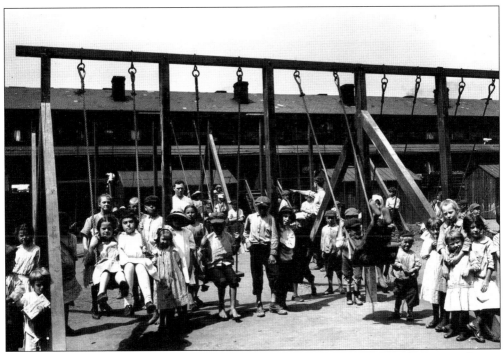

This photograph depicts a playground behind the tenement buildings of Superior Street. Whether the kids are wearing shoes or not, they all seem to be having a good time.

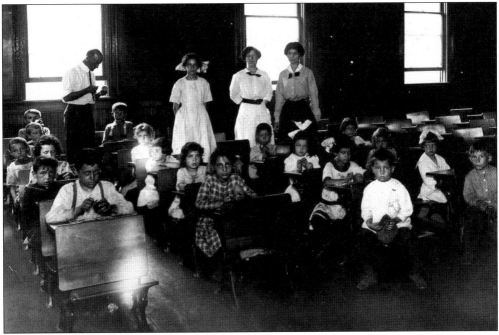

Even before the advent of what is known today as mentoring, the Carnegie Steel Company believed that it had a responsibility to play a positive role in the community, especially with the town's youth. It initiated such programs as Scouting, gardening education, and training in skills such as cooking, knitting, and crafting.

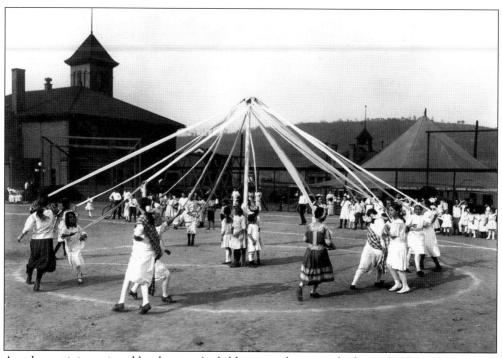

Another activity enjoyed by the town's children was the maypole dance, held beside city hall.

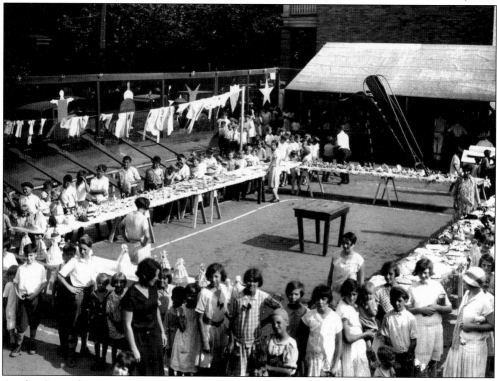

At the Second Street playground, a craft exhibition and contest gave children a chance to proudly display their projects. Prizes were awarded in specific categories.

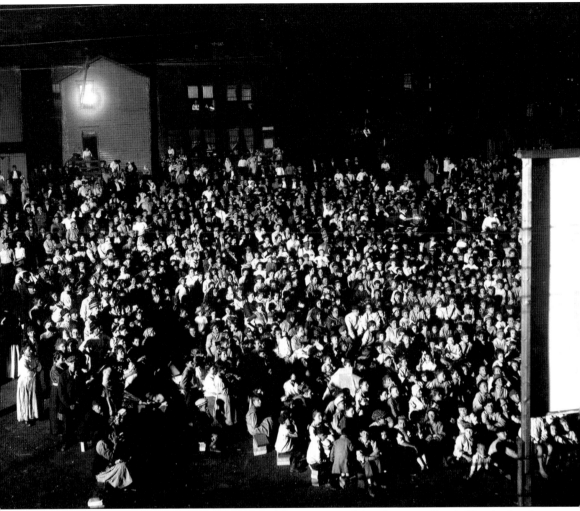

This 1914 photograph shows an evening of fun sponsored by Carnegie Steel. Hundreds of children and adults are gathered to watch movies shown on a makeshift screen in the park. In addition to the movies, the citizens were treated to refreshments and snacks. In the days long before television and video games, seeing a movie was a popular pastime and a cheap date on Saturday nights.

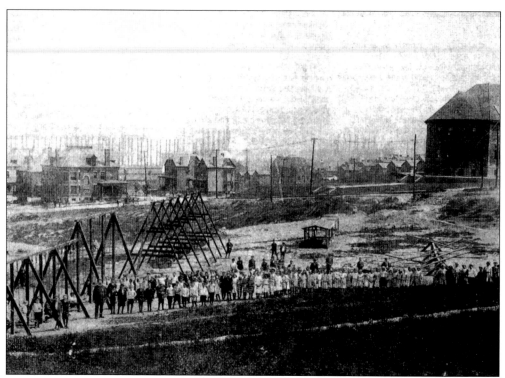

This 1905 photograph shows children gathered in the field across from the library. By 1915, this field had become home to city hall, a three-story apartment building, the Duquesne High School, and a large recreation area featuring swings and a ball field.

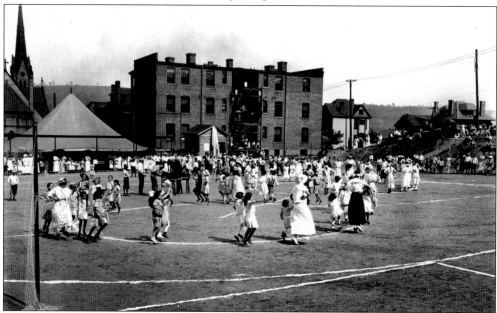

One of the 1914 Field Day activities included a dance contest. The photograph shows older children dancing with partners, while toddlers dance with parents to music played from a phonograph in the middle of the field.

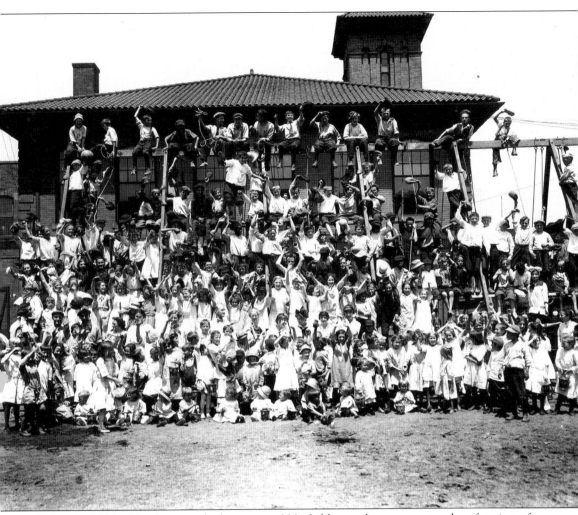

Taken in 1914, this photograph shows over 200 children, who represent only a fraction of the youth who lived in the Second Ward. Carnegie Steel and its workers built playgrounds and recreation areas in all of the town's neighborhoods and wards for the children of Duquesne to enjoy. By the early 1920s, the mill had hired community-based employees who acted as social workers. Their role with the company was to assist mill employees and their families in times of distress, such as an illness or a death in the family. One of the more well-known individuals who worked in this capacity was Laura Bacon. She was killed in 1936 while in service to her community.

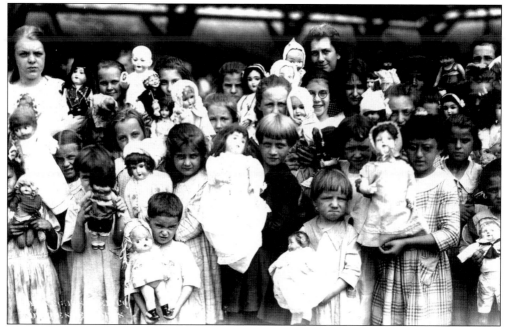

It seemed that no matter what the reason, children were always eager to pose for a photograph. The Carnegie Steel Company's photography department often took sole responsibility for capturing the town's festivities and events; the cost of cameras and the processing of film was usually beyond the means of the common citizen.

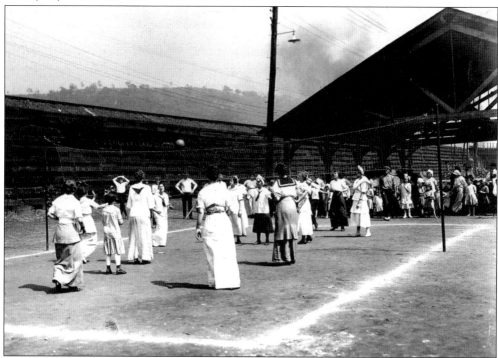

A community volleyball game is enjoyed by children and adults alike at the Superior Street playground.

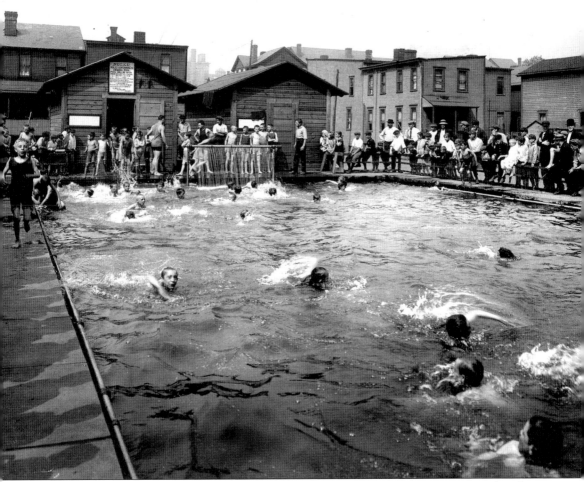

As well as being the town's chief employer, the Carnegie Steel Company was committed to the community and was actively involved in the town's events and functions. Through its welfare program, Carnegie Steel took an active role in the community by building playgrounds and swimming pools. Shown here are children from below the tracks enjoying a cool swim on a hot summer day.

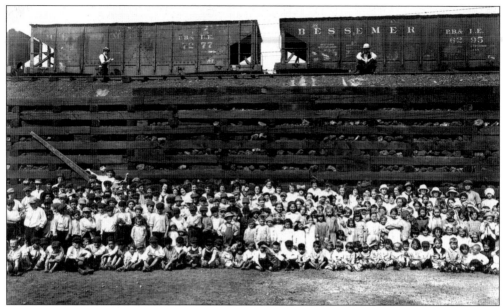

Pictured here are dozens of children stopping to pose for a photograph at a field on Water Street. Not far from the children are the railroad cars that constantly transported material to and from the mill. Many of the town's playgrounds and recreation areas were just feet away from the dangers of the mill.

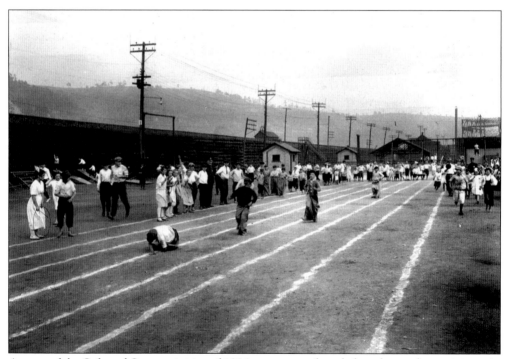

As part of the Safe and Sane activities of 1914, youngsters from below the tracks participate in a sack race, while their friends and families cheer them on. Although prizes awaited only the top finishers, everyone had a good time.

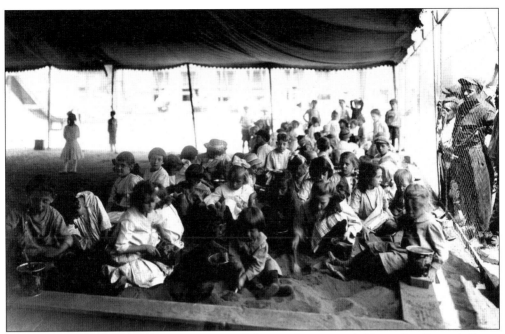

In addition to the swings, teeter-totters, slides, and activity field at the Second Street playground, a gigantic sandbox was constructed for the children to enjoy. To assist in the building of great castles, each child was even given his or her own bucket.

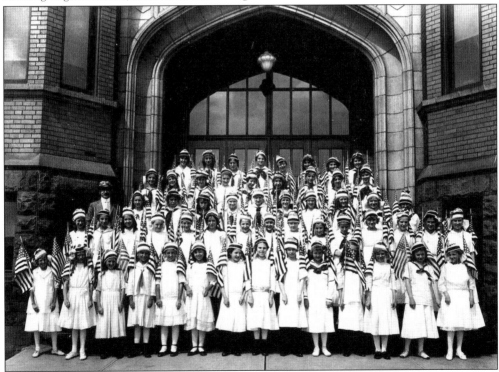

With their own Stars and Stripes to wave in celebration, these pretty young ladies participated in a huge community parade in commemoration of the Fourth of July in 1914.

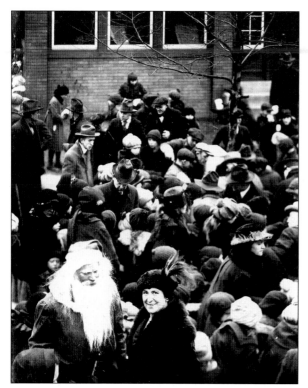

Christmas was always the favorite holiday for the residents of Duquesne. Despite the varied ethnic backgrounds and traditions of the townspeople, the sights, sounds, and smells of the holidays were special to all. Pictured here, people gather in front of the library to meet Santa Claus.

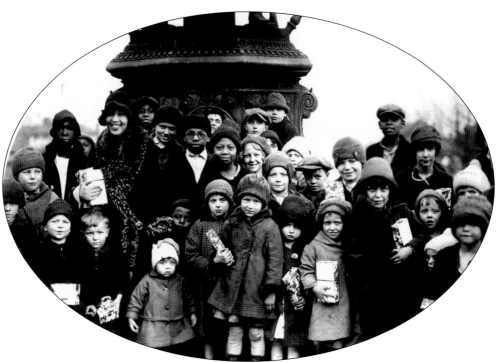

Thanks to the Carnegie Steel Company, its employees, and the town's many civic organizations, no child in Duquesne was ever left without a gift from Santa.

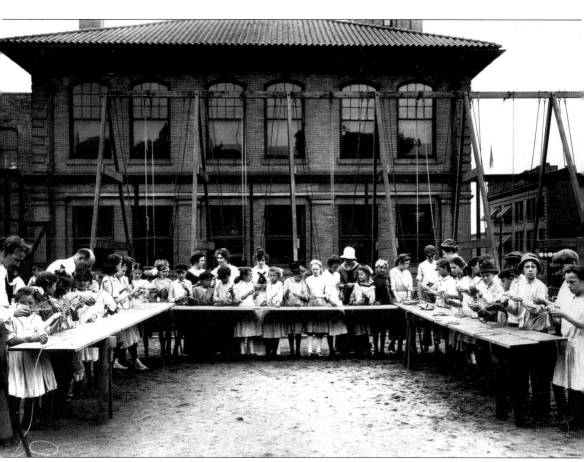

Although there were many activities such as games and sporting events for the children to participate in, the youth of Duquesne were sometimes put to work. Tradition held that when a new furnace was constructed in the mill, the torch of the furnace was lit by a child. In June 1896, the No. 1 furnace was lit by the daughter of the Carnegie Steel Company president. In October of that year, the No. 2 furnace was lit by the daughter of the company treasurer. In May 1897, the daughter of the assistant to the president lit the No. 3 furnace, and No. 4 was lit in June of that year by the son of the superintendent of the Duquesne Works.

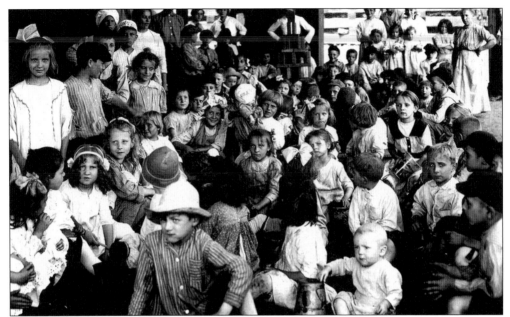

Rich or poor, American-born or foreign, people came to Duquesne to work and raise their families, bringing with them the hopes of prosperity and a bright future for their children. Whether those children were adorned in fancy dresses with ribbons and pigtails or their attire was tattered and they lacked shoes, the promise of a great future in Duquesne could be seen in all of their faces.

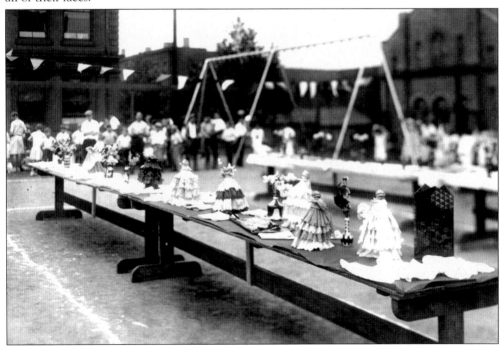

As a testament to the moral character of the residents of this community, valuable knickknacks and precious personal belongings were often displayed at various events and left unattended without fear of loss or theft.

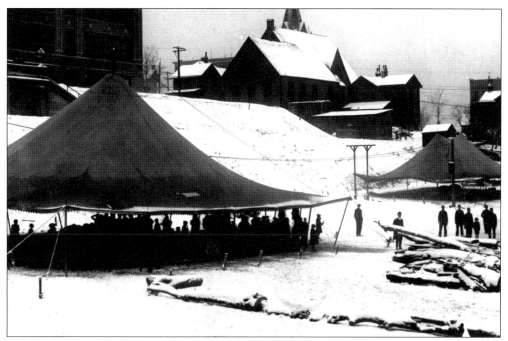

Cold and snowy conditions did not curb the enthusiasm for winter activities in Duquesne. Sledding was a popular pastime, and other outdoor activities included bonfires with hot chocolate for the kids, as pictured here.

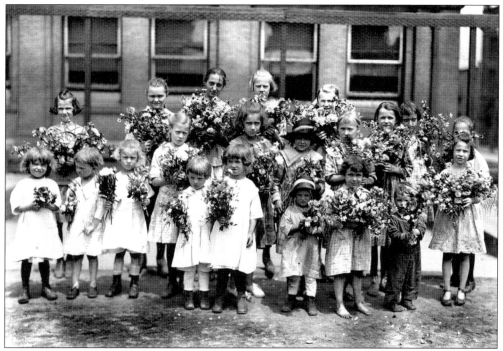

Duquesne was a town of many parades and events. These events included Safe and Sane (a Fourth of July celebration), Field Day, the children's garden exhibition, and the annual Flower Day (shown here).

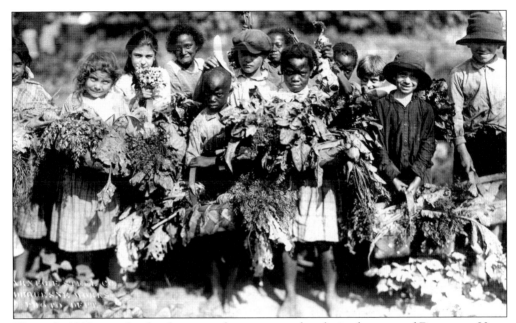

The early 1900s saw the development of many green thumbs in the town of Duquesne. Here, children proudly display for the photographer the varied vegetables and crops grown and cultivated in one of the many community gardens.

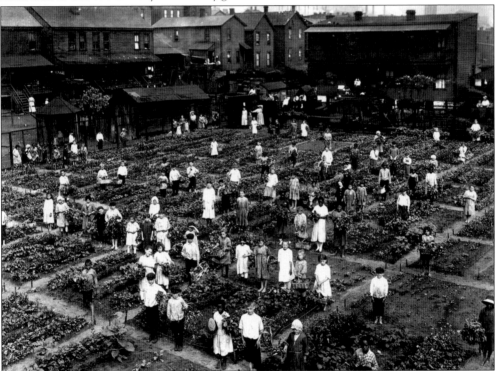

Here is another example of the success of the Carnegie Steel Company's beautification project. What were once empty dirt fields were turned into abundant vegetable gardens that fed dozens of families.

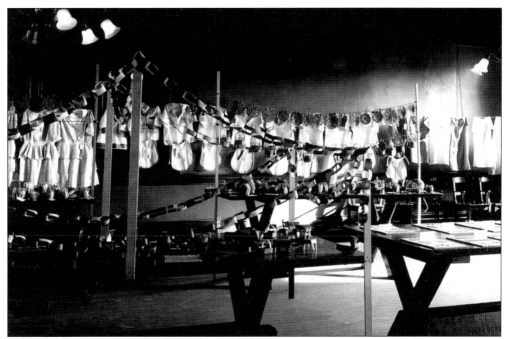

At any of the community events, children and adults alike were encouraged to make, display, and sell crafts and goods. Representing the varied ethnic backgrounds in the community, these displays surely made for wonderful and interesting sights.

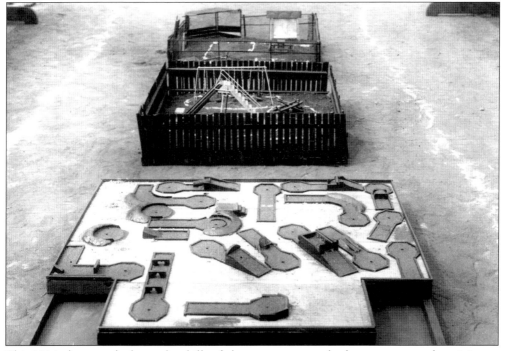

This 1914 photograph shows the skills of clever youngsters who have constructed a miniature baseball field, a small miniature golf course, and a miniature playground complete with a teeter-totter, swings, and a slide.

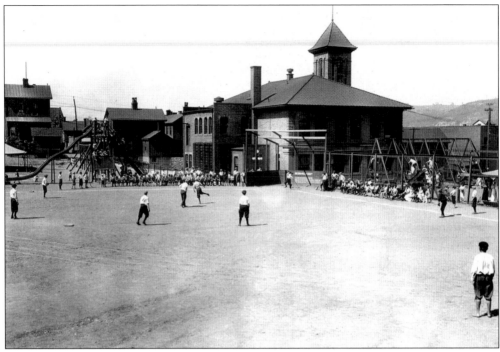

America's favorite pastime was enjoyed by the youth of Duquesne. As part of the Second Street playground, some type of a baseball backstop stood in this field for more than half a century.

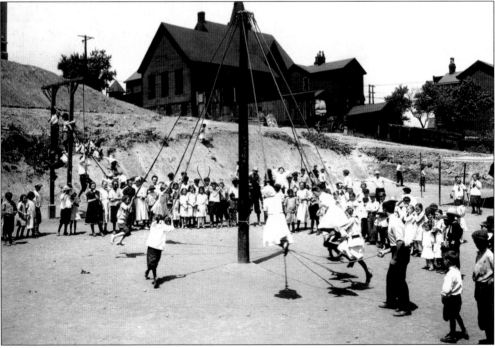

The youth of Duquesne played together without care as their parents worked in the mill, on the railroad, as merchants, and as homemakers, all laboring to make this community a better place to live and to raise a family.

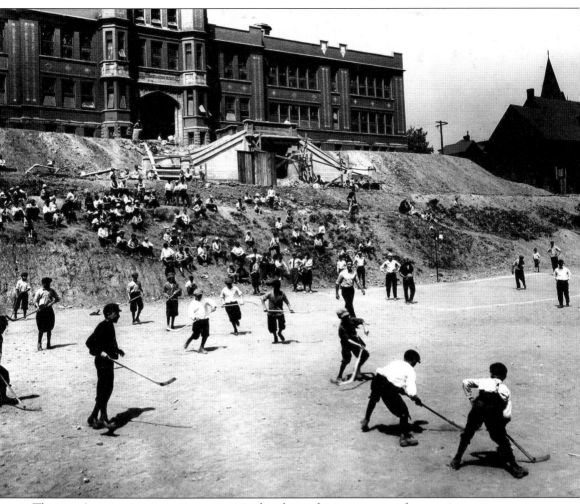

The town's recreation organizers recognized early on the importance of promoting team sports among the youth in the community. Although Duquesne's population consisted of families from all walks of life and language barriers were evident, working together to achieve a common goal was an ideal that was shared in the factories and fostered in the playgrounds. This photograph shows yet another sport that utilized the field behind city hall. The children play street hockey, also known as shinny, using wooden sticks. Although it is not evident in the photograph, the puck was probably a ball.

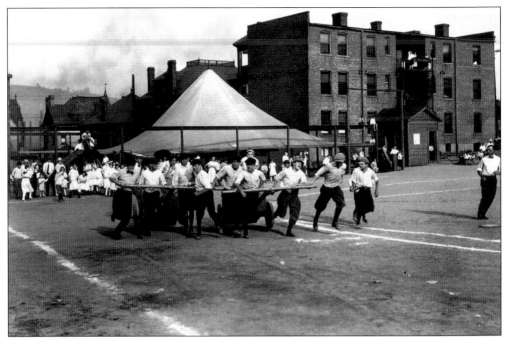

While fun was had by boys and girls alike during the Field Day festivals, not all could participate in the same activities. Shown here, two teams of boys compete in a race while pulling heavy chariot-style carts around a track.

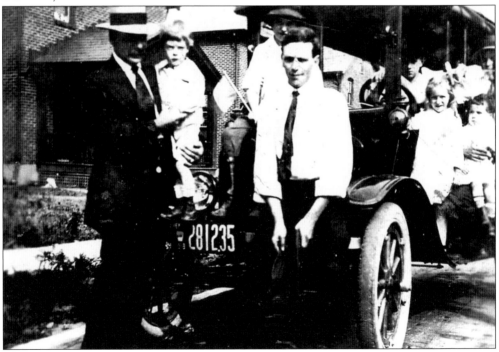

Even with all of the events, activities, games, and sports Duquesne had to offer, sometimes the most fun thing to do was to get in a car and go for a Sunday ride. The first automobile seen in town was driven by Dr. Speer on November 28, 1899.